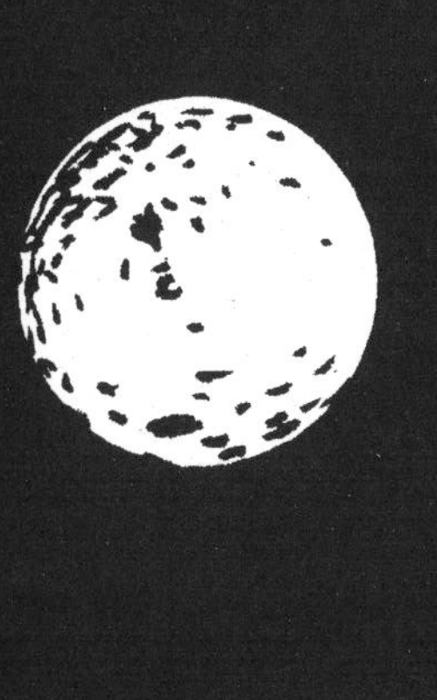

D0292748

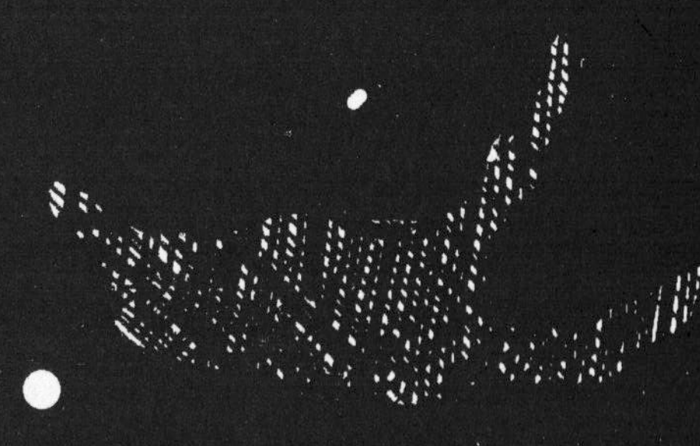

OUR EXPANDING UNIVERSE

by
ALEX
ROBINSON

TOP SHELF
PRODUCTIONS

Published by
Top Shelf Productions
PO Box 1282
Marietta, GA 30061-1282
USA

Editor-in-Chief: Chris Staros

Top Shelf Productions is an imprint of IDW Publishing, a division of Idea and Design Works, LLC. Offices: 2765 Truxin Road, San Diego, CA 92106. Top Shelf Productions®, the Top Shelf logo, Idea and Design Works®, and the IDW logo are registered trademarks of Idea and Design Works, LLC.

Edited by Chris Staros and Leigh Walton with Zac Boone
Design by Chris Ross.

Visit our online catalog at www.topshelfcomix.com.

Printed in Korea.

ISBN 978-1-60309-377-4

18 17 16 15 5 4 3 2 1

BROOKLYN, NEW YORK.

NINE DAYS AGO
UP

HOW OLD DO YOU THINK THOSE GIRLS ARE?

THREE aces!

WHICH ONES? OVER ON THE TABLES?

YEAH. THAT ONE IN THE RED? SHIT!

HM? OH, NO, I WAS GUESSING HOW LONG YOU'LL GO TO THE PEN FOR OGLING TEENAGE GIRLS.
HA HA. IT'S NOT MY FAULT THAT WE LIVE IN A SOCIETY THAT SEXUALIZES YOUNG GIRLS.
PLUS, ALL THE HORMONES AND SHIT THEY PUT IN MILK?
COME ON, SCOTTY, WHERE ARE YOU?
DID HE TEXT YOU ABOUT BEING LATE OR ANYTHING?
HAVE YOU SEEN ANY OF THOSE REALITY SHOWS ABOUT TODDLER BEAUTY PAGEANTS? IT'S FUCKING DISGUSTING.
WE'RE LIVING IN ANCIENT ROME, BILLY.
YOU THINK HE'LL BAIL? THIS IS WHY WE NEED A FOURTH PERSON-- AS A BACK-UP FOR SITUATIONS LIKE THIS.
WHAT ABOUT LARRY?
HE'S AN ASSHOLE. IT'S FINE WITH ME IF WE DON'T PLAY. MY BACK IS KILLING ME.
ALSO, DON'T SHOOT BASKETS WITH THE KICK BALL. IT'S DISRESPECTFUL.

HEY, GUYS! SORRY I'M LATE!
COME ON, BRAIDEN!
THXPLK!
HEY, TOUGH GUY! HOW'S IT GOIN'??
HEY, SCOTTY. DID YOU TELL US YOU WERE BRINGING..?
OH, NO. IT'S JUST FOR A FEW MINUTES. RITU'S PICKING HIM UP FOR ART CLASS. SHE SHOULD BE HERE IN A SEC.
GREAT! LET'S GET GOING. I CALL "ACE!"
HEY, SPORT! YOU READY TO PLAY WITH US? YOU READY TO ENTER THE BATTLE GRID??
GIGGLE! SHRIEK!
CHEPXTKS!! SKEEPLE!!
HA HA!
SO...
WHAT TIME SHOULD SHE BE HERE?
SHOULD WE START OR..?

RITU GOT OUT AT SIX SO SHE SHOULD BE HERE ANY MINUTE.
I CAN TEXT HER TO SEE IF SHE'S RUNNING LATE.
DON'T WORRY ABOUT IT, SCOTTY, WE CAN WAIT.
BESIDES, BROWNIE NEEDS TO SAVE HIS BACK.
EAST DILLON
WE COULD JUST PLAY ONE-ON-ONE WHILE WE WAIT.
THAT'S FINE, YOU GUYS PLAY.
BOUNCE!
BOUNCE!
SO THERE'S THIS NEW OFFICE ADMIN AT SCHOOL -- LOOKS EXACTLY LIKE JOANNE.
OH, YEAH? YOUR JOANNE?
BOUNCE!
WHEN I FIRST SAW HER I WAS LIKE "OH, SHIT, IS THAT..??" BUT ONCE I GOT CLOSE UP THE ILLUSION FADED.

"IT'S FREAKY BECAUSE SHE IS A DEAD RINGER FOR JOANNE-- BUT JOANNE FROM THIRTEEN YEARS AGO, FROM WHEN WE BROKE UP."

WOW. BUT IT'S DEFINITELY NOT HER.
NO, NO. CLOSE UP I COULD SEE. HER NAME IS--

MOMMY!
FROGGY!
WHEW.
HI, GUYS! SORRY I'M LATE!

SMEK!
ROUGH DAY?
UGH, YOU DO NOT UNDERSTAND!
SMEK
OOH, MOMMY CAN'T PICK YOU UP RIGHT NOW, FROGGY!
GRXABITL!!
SHRIEK!
HI, RITU. MAN, I CAN'T BELIEVE HOW BIG HE'S GETTING.

HAHA! EVERY TIME WE TURN AROUND YOU'RE GETTING BIGGER AND BIGGER, AREN'T YOU?
HA, YEAH, SHE'S BEEN SUPER BUSY AT THE OFFICE.
BOUNCE! BOUNCE! BOUNCE! BOUNCE!
AREN'T YOU, BRAIDEN?
HOW'S MARCY? WHEN ARE YOU GUYS COMING OVER FOR THAT DINNER WE OWE YOU?
MOMMY! MOMMY! PAGOTX!!

OKAY, HONEY, WE'LL GO PAINT NOW.
WE'LL LEAVE YOU BOYS TO YOUR KICKBALL CHAMPIONSHIP, THEN.
SEE YOU AT HOME, SCOTT.

OKAY, I'LL BE HOME AROUND TEN, PROBABLY.
BYE, FROGGY! BY-Y-YE!
BOX BALL.
OKAY, I CALL "ACE."

BOUNCE! BOUNCE! BOUNCE!

BOUNCE!

CLUNK

IF I WASN'T MARRIED I WOULD TOTALLY FALL IN LOVE WITH PAM.
TXT FROM: RITU Have Fun! Pick up milk!
PAM WAITRESS PAM?

WHAT, YOU DON'T THINK SHE'S CUTE?
OOH! BROWNIE! YOU SHOULD TOTALLY ASK HER FOR HER NUMBER!
FOR HER "DIGITS!"
HAHA, RIGHT.
ASIDE FROM THE CLICHÉ CHEESINESS OF ASKING OUT YOUR WAITRESS, IT'S--
SHE'S A CUTE GIRL BRINGING YOU ALCOHOL, OF COURSE YOU ARE IN LOVE WITH HER! THAT'S HOW THEY GET TIPS.

AW, SHOOT, I JUST REMEMBERED THAT I CAN'T MAKE NEXT MONTH.
THE NANNY'S GOING HOME TO EL SALVADOR THAT WEEK.

GOD, EL SALVADOR! REMEMBER THE EIGHTIES?
THAT'S OKAY, I THINK MARCE AND I WILL BE OUT OF TOWN ANY WAY.
THE WEEK AFTER?

YOU GUYS ARE GOING AWAY AGAIN?
DIDN'T YOU JUST GET BACK FROM VEGAS?

RENO, ACTUALLY. WHAT CAN I TELL YOU, SCOTTY? WE'RE JET-SETTERS!
BESIDES, THIS TRIP IS TO OCEAN CITY WITH HER FAMILY, IT DOESN'T COUNT.

RITU AND I HAVEN'T BEEN ABLE TO GET AWAY IN AGES. IT WOULD BE GREAT TO GO SOMEWHERE BEFORE THE BABY GETS HERE BUT IT DOESN'T LOOK LIKE THAT WILL HAPPEN.

WOULD YOU AND MARCY HURRY UP AND PROCREATE ALREADY?? THEN WE COULD ALL GO TOGETHER!

DON'T YOU THINK IT WOULD BE KINDA COOL TO GO OUT WITH A STALKER?
EAST DILLON

OKAY, I'LL BITE: WHAT?
SOMEONE IS STALKING YOU?
I'M NOT SURE WHERE TO EVEN PUT THE EMPHASIS IN THAT SENTENCE, I ADMIT.

I KNOW STALKERS GET A BAD RAP AND ALL THAT BUT IF I HAD ONE? AND SHE WAS DECENT LOOKING?
I'D BE TEMPTED. IT WOULD BE, LIKE, FLATTERING, RIGHT?
EAST DILLON

HA! YEAH, UNTIL YOU WANTED TO BREAK UP!

TRUE, BUT BREAK-UPS ALWAYS SUCK.
WOULDN'T IT BE... REFRESHING TO NOT HAVE TO DO ALL THAT FIRST-DATE-BURGEONING-RELATIONSHIP BULLSHIT?
COME ON!

YOU HAVEN'T BURGEONED A GIRL IN AGES, BROWNIE.
TRYING TO TRICK SOME GIRL INTO LIKING YOU BY PRETENDING TO BE SOMEONE YOU AREN'T...
(OR AT LEAST AN IDEALIZED VERSION OF YOU.)

WITH A STALKER IT'S LIKE "SOLD!" YOU KNOW THEY LIKE YOU OUT OF THE BOX!

I'LL HAVE THE McGREEVY BURGER. NO ONIONS, PLEASE.

AND ANOTHER ROUND!

UH... THE TUNA MELT.

OH, AND ONE MORE.

GIVE ME THE PO'BOY.

I'LL ALSO GET A PILSNER. PLEASE.

THANKS.

OKAY, BOYS, BE RIGHT BACK WITH YOUR DRINKS.

THANK YOU, PAM.

TRUE.
MMM.

WHEN I WAS IN SCHOOL I WENT OUT WITH THIS CRAZY GIRL FOR A SHORT TIME.
SHE WAS REALLY CUTE BUT ALSO, LIKE, SERIOUSLY CRAZY, LIKE, CUTTING HERSELF AND SHIT.

RIGHT! I REMEMBER HER! SHIT, WHAT HAPPENED?
"I DON'T KNOW. WE BROKE UP AFTER SHE TOLD ME SHE WAS SLEEPING WITH HER WOMEN'S STUDIES T.A."
WAITWAIT WAITWAIT:
YOU DATED A HOT, BISEXUAL CRAZY GIRL??
FUCK YOU!

IN MY EXPERIENCE "CRAZY" AND "BISEXUAL" IS KIND OF REDUNDANT.
IT WAS COLLEGE! THAT'S WHAT COLLEGE IS FOR!
ONE TIME THIS GIRL CAME OUT TO ME ON A DATE.

HAHA! OH, GOD!
WHAT HAPPENED?

WELL, IT WASN'T GOING SO GREAT, SO-- IT WASN'T A DISASTER, BUT IT WAS CLEAR IT WASN'T A LOVE CONNECTION, Y'KNOW?
UM... THE THING IS... I THINK I'M ... I MIGHT BE, UM, BE A... MIGHT BE GAY.

"IT WAS KIND OF A RELIEF FOR BOTH OF US."
"THE FUNNY THING IS THAT AFTER THAT WE JUST TALKED AND, Y'KNOW, RODE OUT THE CLOCK AND BY THE END I REALLY LIKED HER."

"I GUESS SHE WAS STILL NEW TO THE WHOLE LESBIAN THING. I WAS ONLY THE THIRD PERSON SHE TOLD."

MAN, WHAT IS IT ABOUT US THAT DRIVES WOMEN INTO THE ARMS OF OTHER WOMEN?
HONESTLY, THEY PROBABLY FIND OUR RUGGED MAN-HOOD TOO INTIMIDATING.

I ALWAYS REMEMBER THAT TIME WE WENT TO LUKE'S BACHELOR PARTY IN LONG ISLAND CITY.
RIGHT! WHAT WAS THAT PLACE CALLED?

SEXCALIBUR OR SOMETHING?

NO, UH... (WHAT WAS IT...)

XXXCELSIORS!

SO WE'RE AT THIS BACHELOR PARTY AND, I DON'T KNOW, IT FELT LIKE THE GIRLS WERE BEING REALLY, LIKE, AGGRESSIVE...

HOW YOU DOIN', HONEY?

YOU WANNA DANCE, BABY?

"IT WAS KIND OF OFF-PUTTING."

"BY THE TIME THE SIXTH OR SEVENTH GIRL CAME UP I WAS ALL LIKE...

HEY, HONEY, DO YOU WANT ME TO--

YEAH, I DON'T HAVE ANY MONEY.

OH, OKAY.

"FROM HER TONE YOU COULD TELL SHE WAS KINDA WOUNDED..."

SO... WHAT'S YOUR NAME?

ME? UH, JIM.

JIM... STEELE.

HA HA!

I'M DEMI.

WHAT DO YOU DO FOR A LIVING, "JIM?"

"I FORGET HOW IT STARTED BUT NEXT THING YOU KNOW SHE'S TELLING ME ABOUT HERSELF..."

AS SHE TALKED I LOOKED AT HER FACE AND NOTICED SHE WAS A LITTLE OLDER THAN MOST OF THE OTHER STRIPPERS.
GOING FOR M REAL ESTATE LICENSE. I THE EXAM IN JUNE...
SHE WASN'T OLD OLD -- SHIT, SHE WAS PROBABLY ONLY THIRTY!
I PICKED UP SUBTLE DETAILS... THE FAINT LINES AROUND HER EYES... THE LITTLE HAIRS ON HER ARM...
IN PHOENIX FOR A WHILE BUT MOVED BACK IN '96. IT WAS JUST TOO DARN HO YOU KNOW?
WAS SHE WEARING THAT LINGERIE TO DISGUISE HOW OLD SHE WAS? MAYBE SHE'D HAD A KID OR SOMETHING. WHO KNOWS?
BUT IT MADE ME FEEL SORT OF PROTECTIVE OF HER.
WAS SHE HAPPY FOR A BREAK FROM THE GROPING HORNDOGS?
USING A DIFFERENT TACTIC TO GET ME TO OPEN MY WALLET?
MAYBE BY TALKING LIKE REAL HUMAN BEINGS SHE WAS PROVING TO ME -- OR TO HERSELF -- SHE WASN'T THE SHARK I ASSUMED SHE WAS.
BY THE TIME SHE WALKED AWAY TEN MINUTES LATER I'D FALLEN COMPLETELY IN LOVE WITH HER. "DEMI."

SO, I GUESS WE'VE LEARNED THAT I FALL FOR WOMEN WHO BRING ME FOOD AND BEER...
BROWNIE GOES FOR THE CLOSETED LESBIAN TYPE AND SCOTTY IS INTO GRANNIES WITH HAIRY ARMS!
TO DIVERSITY, THEN!
I'M NOT GOING TO LET YOU CHEAPEN WHAT DEMI AND I HAD THAT NIGHT.

ANYONE UP FOR HITTING FUNCLE'S ON THE WAY HOME?
MMM... NO, I GOTTA HEAD HOME.
AWWW! LET'S E-MAIL ABOUT NEXT MONTH.
OKAY, SEE YOU GUYS.
LATER, SCOTT.
BYE.

MAN, THAT POOR SCHMUCK. EVEN IN HIS FANTASY LIFE HE'S PUSSY-WHIPPED!
DELI
532
534
HAHA! WHAT?

THAT STORY WITH THE STRIPPER? THE OLDER STRIPPER WHO MIGHT'VE HAD A KID? IT'S LIKE RITU PLANTED THAT MEMORY IN HIS HEAD.
THAT'S THE KIND OF FANTASY WOMEN WISH GUYS HAD!
FOOTBALL

OR MAYBE HE'S JUST BEING HONEST AND HE GOES FOR THAT MATERNAL TYPE.

BESIDES, THE POINT OF THE STORY WAS THAT IT WAS ONLY AFTER HE MADE A GENUINE CONNECTION WITH HER AS A PERSON THAT HE WAS ABLE TO GET A BONER.
YOU ONCE HAD EMOTIONS, YOU SHOULD GET THAT.

PSSH!
WHAT HAS GENUINE CONNECTION WITH A PERSON DONE FOR ME LATELY?
AFTER YOU...
FUNCLES!
·NOVELTIES·AMUSEMENTS·

SPEAKING OF HEARTLESS AUTOMATONS, I READ YOUR REVIEW OF THAT NEW ZOMBIE GAME FOR THE XBOX.
IT SOUNDS AMAZING.
IT IS. IT'S GOING TO BE HUGE.

IS SOMEONE STILL MANUFACTURING PAC-MAN KEY CHAINS? OR DO YOU THINK THERE'S SOME "RAIDERS OF THE LOST ARK" WAREHOUSE SOMEWHERE PACKED WITH--
...

AGENT X35
AGENT

THAT VENTRILOQUIST DUMMY. I TOTALLY HAD THAT ON MY CHRISTMAS LIST IN, I DON'T KNOW, SECOND GRADE? THIRD GRADE?
FROM THE SEARS CATALOGUE.
I COMPLETELY FORGOT IT EXISTED UNTIL THIS VERY MOMENT.

I AM 100% SINCERE WHEN I SAY YOU SHOULD BUY THAT DUMMY.
AND GET MATCHING SUITS.
EAST DILLON
FOOTBALL

WELL, I'M 75% SINCERE WHEN I SAY THAT MARCY WOULD KILL ME.
KILL YOU FOR BUYING KENNY TALK!
I TAKE IT BACK: SCOTTY ISN'T THE WHIPPED ONE.

HUH? OH, NO, IT'S NOT THAT.
WE'RE TRYING TO GET RID OF A BUNCH OF STUFF AS IT IS. BOOKS AND CLUTTER.
PBLBLPBLBT!!
Game
SHE WOULDN'T BE HAPPY IF I BROUGHT MORE JUNK INTO THE APARTMENT, Y'KNOW?

I DON'T GET IT: WHY IS SHE MAKING YOU GET RID OF ALL YOUR BOOKS AND SHIT?
CRAP! LOOK: MICRONAUTS!

SHE'S NOT MAKING ME. WE JUST NEED TO CLEAR SOME SPACE, THAT'S ALL.
ARE YOU ALMOST DONE? I HAVE TO--
BUTTONS 25¢
BUTTONS 25¢

WAIT: MORE SPACE?
WHY DO YOU GUYS NEED MORE..
99¢ Candy BOMBS!
candy BOMBS
WORMS
EAST DILLON
FOOTBALL

OH.

"OKAY, DAWG, SEE YOU NEXT TIME."
"YEAH, HIT ME ON THE I.M. TOMORROW."
"OKAY. HAVE FUN DOWN AT THE SHORE."
G

MILK

IT'S THE PLUMBER. I'VE COME TO FIX THE SINK.
OH! HEY, SWEETIE! HOW'D IT GO?
HAVE FUN WITH THE BOYS?
GEEK LOVE

YEAH, I KICKED BUTT. Heh, I'M A LITTLE BUZZED.
OOH, I'M SO JEALOUS!
I PICKED UP SOME MILK.
I'M GONNA PEEK IN ON FROGGY AND BE RIGHT BACK.
DID HE GIVE YOU ANY TROUBLE?

NO, HE MISSED YOU, THOUGH.
WELL, THANKS FOR THE PASS. I OWE YOU ONE.

CREEHR

mmmrawr.

MR. BELVEDERE!

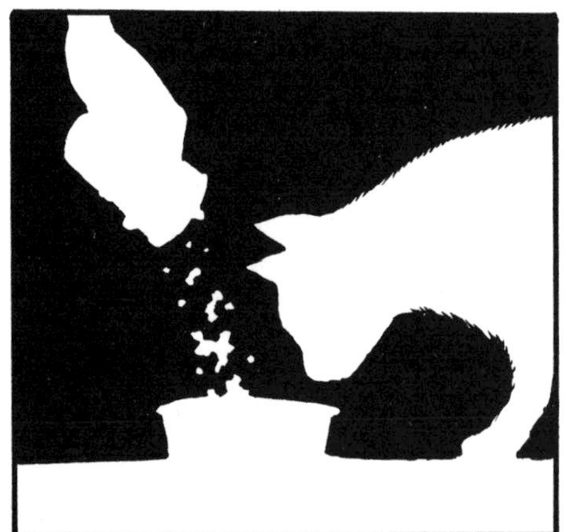

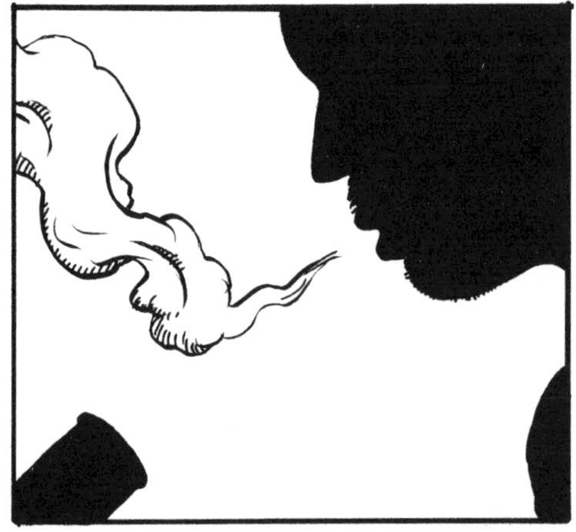

sure you don't re
ne but my name is Mich
nd went to high school t
O WILDCATS! LOL!!) . An
s browsing at the Strand
behold I pick up a book
BURGER STEAK! I
ssed! It'

MARCY?

HEY, TOUGH GUY! HEY TOUGH GUY!

RAHR! RAHR! YES!

SNORT! GRRRFFLE!

HEY, BABY! HOW'D IT GO?

WERE YOU RIGHT? DID SCOTTY BAIL?

NO, HE WAS LATE BUT WE HAD FUN. RITU CAME BY AND ASKED ABOUT GOING OUT TO DINNER.
GOING OUT? REALLY? WOW, I'LL E-MAIL HER TOMORROW.

DOES CHOPS NEED TO GO POOPIES?
NOPE! I TOOK HIM OUT ALREADY! SO...

I WAS SITTING WAITING FOR YOU TO COME HOME SO WE COULD INDULGE IN A LITTLE, EH... SNUGGLETHON.

IN FACT, I HOPE YOU DON'T MIND BUT, Hee Hee, I SORT OF STARTED WITHOUT YOU...
WOW! OKAY! WELL, LET ME FRESHEN UP MY BEER BREATH AND I'LL JOIN YOU! Heh!
OKAY, BUT HURRY UP, SILLY BILLY...
ACCORDING TO MY CALCULATIONS I'M AT THE PERFECT TIME IN MY CYCLE FOR YOU TO PLANT YOUR SEED...
SHIKA SHIKA SHIKA
I CAN JUST FEEL THAT EGG EAGERLY WAITING FOR YOUR BOYS TO COME A-KNOCKIN', YOU KNOW?
SPIT

BABY, UH...
I'M ACTUALLY...
BETWEEN THE BOXBALL AND THE DRINKING I FEEL KINDA WIPED, SO, UH, I DON'T KNOW IF I'M UP, UH, FOR ANY, UH, SNUGGLING.
REALLY?
IS THERE ANYTHING I CAN DO TO, LIKE, CHANGE YOUR MIND?
PENCEY

I'M SORRY, MARCE. HOW ABOUT TOMORROW?
I PROMISE I'LL GIVE YOU TWO HELPINGS OF MY WHITE HOT MAN SEED.
UGH! GUH-ROSS!
OW! HAHA!
FUMPF!
PENCEY

DO YOU WANT TO WATCH JON STEWART?
OH! THAT'S RIGHT: NEIL DEGRASSI TYSON IS ON.
SNOOOORT
CHOPS

YOU AND I AND EVERYONE WE KNOW LIVE IN A FAMILY OF APPROXIMATELY FIFTY GALAXIES KNOWN AS "THE LOCAL GROUP."
EACH OF THESE GALAXIES CONTAINS A FEW BILLION STARS...
...BUT TWO OF THEM -- ANDROMEDA, AND OUR HOME, THE MILKY WAY -- CONTAIN OVER A TRILLION STARS BETWEEN THEM!
THESE TWO GIANTS DOMINATE THE LOCAL GROUP!

THE KIDS REALLY LOVE BILLY.

JIMMY DOESN'T DO MUCH ROUGH-HOUSING, PROBABLY CUZ HE'S SO FUCKING TIRED FROM WORK.

HOW HAVE THINGS BEEN GOING? I KNOW HE WAS HAVING SOME, UH, PERSONNEL STUFF...

YEAH, THEY BROUGHT IN SOME NEW MARKETING DOUCHEBAG AND HE'S BEEN ASSERTING HIS DOMINANCE BY BRINGING IN HIS OWN PEOPLE.
HALF OF JIM'S TEAM HAS BEEN FORCED OUT.
WOW. IS JIM WORRIED, MISS? ARE YOU GUYS GONNA BE OKAY?
WHO KNOWS, MAR?
I GUESS WE'LL GET BY SOMEHOW.
OH, DO ME A FAVOR AND DON'T MENTION THIS TO MOMMY AND DADDY, OKAY?
THEY'RE ALREADY INCLINED TO WORRY AND MEDDLE AS IT IS.
OY, YOU DON'T HAVE TO TELL ME.
SHE'S ALREADY STARTED GOING ON ABOUT--
NO! IT'S MY TURN!
NO, ME!!
TUCKER, IT'S ELIJAH'S TURN, SWEETY.

EVERY FIFTH WORD OUT OF MOMMY'S MOUTH IS HOW SHE WANTS ANOTHER GRANDCHILD.
(MISSY! LOOK AT THIS GUY! LOOK AT THIS GUY!)
CAN YOU GET ME ANOTHER BEER?
THAT DOES BEG THE QUESTION, MAR: WHAT'S THE DEAL? ARE YOU GUYS TRYING OR..?
WELL, YEAH! I GUESS WE KIND OF ARE, SO, YEAH.
IT LOOKS LIKE WE'RE OUT.
SHIT.
I GOT OFF THE PILL A FEW MONTHS BACK SO WE'RE GOING TO SEE WHAT HAPPENS, YOU KNOW?
SO: YEAH, WE'RE TRYING.
HEH.
OKAY!
???
WELL, THANKS, MOM.

DON'T GET PISSY WITH ME, MARCY, I WAS JUST ASKING.
I DON'T GIVE A SHIT IF YOU HAVE KIDS OR NOT.
SORRY, MISS.
I THINK SHE JUST HAS ME ON EDGE ABOUT THE WHOLE THING, AND SOMETIMES I THINK BILLY--
HE...

GOD, WHY DOES THAT HAPPEN?
MOMMY USED TO COMPLAIN ABOUT HOW NANA TREATED HER AND NOW SHE DOES THE EXACT SAME THINGS WITH US, YOU KNOW?
DOESN'T SHE SEE THAT? WHY CAN'T SHE SEE THAT?

SIGH WHO KNOWS?

DO YOU THINK WE'LL DO THE SAME THING TO OUR KIDS?
HMMM. NO.
I THINK IT'S DIFFERENT FOR OUR GENERATION. MOMMY HAD ME WHEN SHE WAS... TWENTY-FIVE? TWENTY-SIX? I CAN'T EVEN IMAGINE HAVING TUCKER WHEN I WAS THAT YOUNG!
BY THE TIME I DID HAVE HIM I WAS THIRTY-FIVE, AN ADULT. I'D TRAVELED, HAD A CAREER.

WE WON'T NEED TO LIVE VICARIOUSLY THROUGH OUR KIDS.
THAT MAKES SENSE, RIGHT?
YEAH, I THINK SO.
BILLY! COME ON IN! WE'RE HEADING BACK!

AHHH...

BILLY, I GOTTA SAY YOU DID A GREAT JOB WEARING OUT THE BOYS.
BEER?
THANKS.
THEY COULD HARDLY KEEP THEIR EYES OPEN AT DINNER.
YEAH, I KNOW HOW THEY FEEL. I'M WIPED OUT MYSELF!
OOH, AND SUNBURNED.

SO, BILL, YOU STILL DOING THE DOG-WALKING THING?
UH, YEAH, PRETTY MUCH, JIM.
HE JUST GOT PROMOTED TO MANAGER!
OH! AND WHAT ABOUT YOU, MARCY? HOW'RE THINGS AT THE HOSPITAL?

MANAGER, HUH? DOES THAT MEAN YOU'RE THE ONE WHO TELLS THE DOGS WHAT TO DO? HEH HEH!
HA HA! YEAH.

UM, YOU KNOW? GOOD ACTUALLY.
I FEEL AS IF MY MUSIC THERAPY IS FINALLY REALLY BEING INTEGRATED INTO THE HOSPITAL.
WE'RE REALLY "CLICKING" FINALLY.

IT'S NOT JUST WALKING, THOUGH. WE DO GROOMING, TRAINING, THAT STUFF.
WE TAKE PEOPLE'S DOGS WHEN THEY GO TO WORK OR ON VACATION.

OOH! TELL MOM ABOUT M.D. GUY.
(YOU'RE GONNA LOVE THIS, MOM)
GASP! DID YOU SAY M.D.??

SAY, THAT'S RIGHT! I HEARD ABOUT THOSE PLACES ON THE NEWS! WHAT DO THEY CALL THEM? "DOGGIE DAY CARE?"
THAT'S RIGHT.
GOSH! WHAT WILL THEY THINK UP NEXT, AM I RIGHT? HAHA!
:SIGH: I DUNNO, RUSS, BILL MIGHT HAVE THE RIGHT IDEA, SITTING AROUND PLAYING WITH DOGS ALL DAY.
AS IT IS I SPEND ALL MY TIME AT THE OFFICE, BUSTING MY HUMP, WORKING LATE, WORKING WEEKENDS...
AND THIS ONE, SHE GIVES ME NOTHING BUT GRIEF, Y'KNOW?
"YOU'RE WORKING TOO MUCH! YOU NEVER SEE THE KIDS!"
:SQUAAAGH!:

DID YOU HEAR ABOUT HEATHER FRANKFORT?
WHY ARE YOU WHISPERING? IS SHE NEXT DOOR OR--
HEATHER FRANKFORT?
MARCY'S FRIEND WITH THE ZITS?
PSORIASIS.
I HAVEN'T TALKED TO HER SINCE HIGH SCHOOL.
WHAT HAPPENED TO HER?

I WAS OVER AT THE I.G.A. AND I BUMPED INTO MRS. O'BRIEN AND SHE TOLD ME THAT HEATHER WAS DIAGNOSED WITH M.S.
CAN YOU BELIEVE IT?

NO OFFENSE, RUSS.
HA, NO, I KNOW MISSY CAN BE A HANDFUL, AND IT'S ALWAYS TOUGH TO BALANCE CAREER AND FAMILY.
HAHA! YOU GOT THAT RIGHT!
WHOA, THAT'S FUCKED UP.
POOR HEATHER.
THAT'S NOT EVEN THE WORST PART!
NOW SHE'S PREGNANT!
ON PURPOSE!
WOW, THAT'S GREAT SHE COULD FIND A GUY WITH ALL THE SKIN ISSUES SHE HAS.

WAIT A MINUTE: DO YOU KNOW WHAT HER CONDITION IS? M.S. CAN TAKE YEARS TO MANIFEST ITSELF, MOM.

SHE MIGHT NOT EVEN --

BUT, HONEY, ISN'T IT... IRRESPONSIBLE TO BRING A CHILD INTO THAT SITUATION?

IT'S LIKE SHE'S PLAYING RUSSIAN ROULETTE: NO ONE KNOWS WHAT'S GOING TO HAPPEN!

THIS GUY AT WORK --

EXACTLY, MOM! THAT'S TRUE FOR EVERYONE! MISSY COULD GET RUN OVER BY A BUS, DOES THAT MEAN SHE SHOULDN'T HAVE HAD KIDS??

HOW DID I GET --

HONEY, THAT'S --

LAH CONSULTING
BLAH BLAH
HA HA!
BLAH BLAH
PROFITS!

BLAH
LAH BLAH
TAXES
LAH

LAH BLAH
RUARTER
LAH BLAH
RM?

HA!
LAH
GENCY
BLAH
LAH
BLAH

BLAH
NSBORG
BLAH

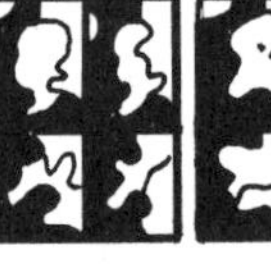

GASP!

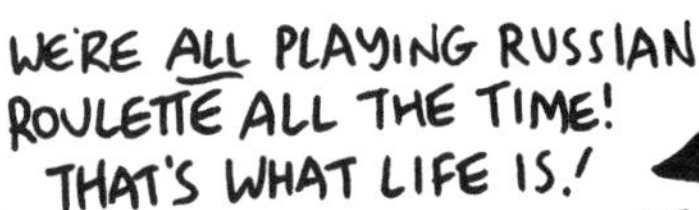
WE'RE ALL PLAYING RUSSIAN ROULETTE ALL THE TIME! THAT'S WHAT LIFE IS!
HORRIBLE THINGS CAN HAPPEN AT ANY TIME: MISSY COULD GET HIT BY A BUS, BILLY COULD BE PUSHED OFF A SUBWAY PLATFORM BY A SORORITY GIRL WHO STOPPED TAKING HER MEDS! I COULD HAVE A GIANT TUMOR FESTERING IN MY..

GASP!
YOU DON'T THINK YOU HAVE A TUMOR--?!

?? NO! I'M--
NO, WAIT, YOU KNOW WHAT? I DON'T KNOW IF I DO AND THAT'S MY POINT!
YOU CAN'T LIVE LIFE NOT DOING STUFF BECAUSE --
BILLY, ARE YOU OKAY?

OH, YEAH, I'M SORRY. I GOT STARTLED WHEN MY PHONE BUZZED, I WAS SO WRAPPED UP IN JIM'S STORY.
I SHOULD TAKE THIS, SORRY.

YEAH, SO... UH... WHERE WAS I?
THERE WAS THIS GUY AT WORK WHO--

RUSSIAN ROULETTE! THAT'S RIGHT!
YEAH, SO I GIVE HEATHER A LOT OF CREDIT. SHE WAS DEALT A BAD HAND BUT SHE'S NOT LETTING THAT STOP HER FROM GETTING WHAT SHE CAN OUT OF LIFE.
MORE POWER TO HER!

WELL, I'M CERTAIN MISSY WILL AGREE THAT YOUR PERSPECTIVE MIGHT CHANGE IF YOU CHOOSE TO BECOME A MOTHER SOME DAY.
UGH, MOM...

...

HOW DID I NOT SEE THIS COMING??

BROWNIE, YOUR TIMING IS IMPECCABLE. WHAT'S UP?

DUDE, GUESS WHERE I AM?

UM... A.C.*?

SHIT! THAT'S SO WEIRD!

NO, I'M AT THE LAUNDROMAT.

*ATLANTIC CITY, N.J.

I DON'T GET IT. WHAT'S SO WEIRD ABOUT THAT?

JUST THAT, OUT OF ALL THE PLACES YOU COULD PICK, YOU WENT WITH ANOTHER COIN-BASED ECONOMY.

WHERE YOU AT? COME HANG OUT.

FIRST OFF, A.C. HASN'T HAD COIN SLOT MACHINES IN A DECADE.

BUT LET ME JUST TELL MY IN-LAWS I'M LEAVING THEIR BEACH HOUSE SO I CAN DRIVE FOUR HOURS TO HANG OUT IN A QUEENS LAUNDROMAT.

OH! RIGHT! I FORGOT YOU GUYS ARE DOWN AT THE SHORE.
HOW'S IT GOING? IS MISSY STILL WITH THAT ASSHOLE JEB?
JIM. GOD, HE'S INSUFFERABLE.
I THOUGHT THAT AFTER ALL THESE YEARS WE HAD AN UNDERSTANDING THAT WE HAD NO COMMON GROUND, RIGHT?
SO WHY DOES HE KEEP TALKING TO ME ABOUT SPORTS AND BUSINESS?
LET IT GO, JIM!
LET MISSY KNOW IF SHE'S READY FOR SOME NO-STRINGS ADULTERY, I JUST HAD MY MATTRESS FUMIGATED.
I'M AT THE POINT WHERE I'M GONNA TELL MARCE WE CAN'T DO THIS AGAIN. THIS RELAXING IS JUST NOT WORTH THE STRESS.
OH, YEAH? LISTEN: GUESS WHO E-MAILED ME RECENTLY.
24
AGAIN WITH THE GUESSING? CAN'T YOU JUST TELL..
MICHELLE SACCO!!
...
I DON'T KNOW WHO THAT IS.

Michelle Sacco
BULLETPOINTS:
• SHE WAS A CLASS BENEATH ME IN HIGH SCHOOL.
• SHE HAD A MAGNIFICENT RACK.
• SHE CONTACTED ME TO LET ME KNOW SHE READ -- AND ENJOYED! -- "HAMBURGER STEAK!"
NO SMOKING
WHAT, YOUR NOVEL? THAT'S COOL!
IT'S MORE THAN COOL! BILLY, HAVING A GIRL YOU HAD A SECRET CRUSH ON IN HIGH SCHOOL READ -- AND ENJOY! -- YOUR NOVEL IS NOTHING SHORT OF THE AMERICAN DREAM!
THE "I'LL SHOW YOU ALL" THEORY OF LITERARY HISTORY.

SO WHAT'S HER DEAL? IS SHE STILL CUTE? IS SHE A FAT HOUSE-WIFE IN DAYTON, OHIO NOW?

"IT'S HARD TO SAY. I SCOURED FIFTEEN DIFFERENT SOCIAL NETWORKS AND COULD ONLY FIND ONE MURKY PHOTO."

BUT SHE SAYS SHE'S LIVING OUTSIDE OF PHILLY, SELLING REAL ESTATE OR SOME BULL-SHIT.
OH, YEAH: SHE'S DIVORCED.
SHE TOLD YOU ALL THAT IN ONE E-MAIL? I DON'T KNOW, BROWNIE, THAT SOUNDS A BIT... DESPERATE.
OH, UH, NO, WE'VE E-MAILED A FEW TIMES.

"A FEW TIMES??" GOOD GOD, MAN, YOU'RE REALLY CONSIDERING THIS, AREN'T YOU?

I...
BILLY, IT'S MICHELLE SACCO.

OKAY, HEH-HEH, I GOTTA RUN. I GET BACK ON SUNDAY BUT KEEP ME POSTED.
SAY HI TO MISSY!

WHAT'S UP? EVERYTHING OKAY?

WOULD YOU BE MAD IF NEXT SUMMER WE SKIPPED THE WHOLE BEACH-HOUSE-WITH-MY-FAMN-DAMILY? MAYBE GO SOMEPLACE NEW?

NEW AND VERY, VERY FAR AWAY? ⁝SIGH⁝

THIS WAS A GREAT IDEA.
I LOVE WALKING ON THE BEACH AT NIGHT.
IT'S LIKE THAT KIDS' BOOK WHERE THEY HIDE OUT AND SPEND THE NIGHT IN THE MUSEUM AFTER IT CLOSES?
IT'S HARD TO BELIEVE IT'S EVEN THE SAME PLACE, RIGHT?
WITHOUT ALL THE SUN AND KIDS AND STUFF?
HA, I'M A LITTLE DRUNK.

I HAVE TO ADMIT I FIND IT KIND OF... UNSETTLING. IT MAKES ME FEEL SO SMALL.
LIKE YOU SAID, DURING THE DAY IT FEELS LIKE THE OCEAN WAS PUT HERE FOR OUR BENEFIT.
LIKE DISNEYWORLD OR CENTRAL PARK.
YOU CAN IMAGINE THEM SHUTTING DOWN THE WAVES WHEN THE LAST SUNBATHERS LEAVE.
BUT AT NIGHT, YOU REALIZE THAT THAT'S JUST HUMAN SPIN. THE OCEAN DOESN'T GIVE A SHIT ABOUT US.
THE TIDE KEEPS ROLLING WHETHER WE'RE HERE OR NOT.
LIKE TIME.
BOY, YOU SURE KNOW HOW TO CHEER ME UP.

HAHA! SORRY. YOU'RE RIGHT.
HEY! LET'S GO SKINNY DIPPING!
WHAT, SERIOUSLY? NOW WHO'S THE DRUNK ONE?
BESIDES, WHAT ABOUT CHOPS? HE CAN'T SWIM!

HE'LL STAY HERE AND GUARD OUR CLOTHES. JUST FOR A FEW MINUTES! C'MON!
IT WILL BE FREEZING! WE'RE KIND OF OLD FOR THIS SORT OF THING, AREN'T WE?
AREN'T YOU WORRIED THE BIG, EVIL OCEAN WILL CONSUME US? HAHA!

EXCUSES, EXCUSES...
I NEVER SAID IT WAS EVIL.. JUST ENORMOUS AND INDIFFERENT. LIKE GOD!

Hee Hee!

WAIT WAIT! HOLD ON A SEC.!
WHAT'S WRONG? IS SOMEONE COMING??

Way Back When
Sigh
THIS IS RIDICULOUS.
GO SAY SOMETHING.
IF AIMEE MANN OR SOMEBODY WAS COMING OVER, WOULD YOU PUT TOGETHER A PLAYLIST THAT INCLUDED SOME OF HER MUSIC?
GREEN DAY
DeGrassi
TEN OTHER COURTS!!
I DON'T MEAN YOU'D ONLY PLAY HER MUSIC.
DO YOU PUT SOME IN THE MIX TO, UH, PROVE YOU LIKE HER MUSIC? LIKE OUT OF RESPECT?
OR WOULD THAT BE AWKWARD?

BEFORE WE GO TOO FAR DOWN THIS RABBIT HOLE: IS THERE ANY CHANCE THIS MIGHT ACTUALLY HAPPEN?
AIMEE MANN COMING OVER, I MEAN.
UMMM.
PROOOOOOOOOOOOOOBABLY....... NOT?
IT'S NOT ENTIRELY UNPOSSIBLE. I MEAN, I KNOW SOME PEOPLE IN THE MUSIC BIZ WHO PROBABLY KNOW HER, OR AT LEAST KNOW PEOPLE WHO KNOW HER.
BUT OTHER THAN THAT LONG SHOT?
I'D SAY THERE'S A ... TWO-PERCENT CHANCE IT WILL HAPPEN.
OKAY. SO IN THIS SCENARIO, WHAT'S THE DEAL? IS IT A ROMANTIC DINNER FOR TWO? AN UNO PARTY? MOVIE NIGHT?
WHAT'S THE CONTEXT, BROWNIE?

PROBABLY A GROUP THING. MAYBE DINNER, MAYBE SOME UNO.
I'M PRETTY SURE SHE'S STILL MARRIED TO SEAN PENN'S BROTHER SO NOT A ROMANTIC DINNER.
I WOULD THINK MUSICIANS WOULD BE SICK OF THEIR OWN SONGS, RIGHT?
THAT'S TRUE. SHE'S PROBABLY PLAYED "LUKA" SIX MILLION TIMES BY NOW.
(HAS SCOTTY TEXTED YOU? HE'S ALWAYS LATE.)
STILL, YOU KNOW THOSE SHOW-BIZ TYPES.
TOTAL EGO-MANIACS. SHE'D PROBABLY BE INSULTED IF YOU DIDN'T THROW IN A FEW TRACKS FROM "MAGNOLIA" AT LEAST.
WHOAWHOAWHOA: "MAGNOLIA??" THAT'S HER MOST POPULAR ALBUM! SHE'D THINK I WAS A TOTAL POSER.
NO, IF I'M DOING THIS I'M GOING WITH A DEEP CUT.
MAYBE AN OBSCURE B-SIDE OR IMPORT ONLY THING.
THAT'S A GOOD TACTIC. GAUGE HER REACTION: IS SHE FLATTERED OR DOES SHE ROLL HER EYES?
GET READY TO JUMP UP AND SKIP TO THE NEXT TRACK, JUST IN CASE.
"OH, SORRY, AIMEE MANN!"

BEHOLD.

AW, MAN. TEN COURTS AND THEY HAVE TO PICK THE ONE WITH THE BOX BALL COURT. WHAT SHOULD WE DO? WAIT?

SO, HOW'D IT GO WITH YOUR HIGH SCHOOL CRUSH, BROWNIE?
DID YOU FINALLY LIVE OUT YOUR TEEN-AGE FANTASY AND GET TO SECOND BASE?
HA, NOT YET. WE HAVEN'T ACTUALLY MET BUT SHE SENT A PICTURE.
WAIT, A HIGH SCHOOL GIRL SENT YOU PICTURES??

NO, I HAVEN'T FALLEN THAT FAR, BUT CLOSE: SHE'S A GIRL I WAS IN LOVE WITH TWENTY YEARS AGO.
WOW, AND YOU GOT BACK IN TOUCH? DOES SHE HOLD UP? SHOW US THE PICTURE!

LET'S SEE... WELL, SHE'S OLDER, BUT SHE'S STILL GOT THAT JE NE COMPRENDS PAS, Y'KNOW?

COOL.
SO, WHAT'S HER DEAL? DO YOU THINK SHE'S TRYING TO "RECONNECT?"

I DON'T KNOW. I MEAN, I'M NOT GOING TO PRETEND THE IDEA DIDN'T CROSS MY MIND OR THAT IT WASN'T MY PRIMARY MOTIVATION FOR WRITING BACK BUT... IT'S WEIRD, ISN'T IT?
WOULD IT BE HER I WAS MAKING SWEET, SWEET LOVE TO, OR MY MEMORY OF HER IN HIGH SCHOOL?
(FANTASY OF HER, REALLY, SINCE I KNEW ALMOST NOTHING ABOUT HER ASIDE FROM WHERE HER LOCKER WAS AND WHICH BUS SHE TOOK.)
IT'S SAFE TO ASSUME SHE MIGHT FEEL THE SAME WAY. WHEN SHE THINKS OF SEAN BROWNLOW SHE PICTURES A RUGGED YOUNG MAN WITH A THICK HEAD OF HAIR.
PANTHERS
SO IF WE DO "RECONNECT" THEN ON SOME LEVEL IT WILL BE MY INNER-TEENAGER DOING IT WITH HER INNER-TEENAGER, BOTH OF US IN FLABBY, MIDDLE-AGED BODIES.
WOW.
IT'S THE MOST DEPRESSING TIME TRAVEL STORY EVER.
I KNOW! THAT'S WHY PART OF ME DOESN'T WANT TO DO IT!
SHE'S BEEN IN MY JERK-OFF FANTASY ROTATION FOR TWENTY YEARS!
I DON'T CARE WHO YOU ARE, NO ONE CAN LIVE UP TO THAT HYPE!

OH, COME ON! YOU HAVE TO AT LEAST GIVE IT A SHOT!
YOUR JERK-OFF BENCH MUST BE DEEP ENOUGH WHERE YOU CAN AFFORD TO RISK ONE GIRL!
BESIDES, WHO KNOWS? YOU MIGHT ACTUALLY, YOU KNOW, LIKE HER.
PSSH! UNLIKELY.
EVERYONE IN MY HIGH SCHOOL WAS A BORING JERK.
GREEN DAY
HOW'D THIS GIRL FIND YOU, ANYWAY? DRUNK FACEBOOK SEARCH?
THAT'S THE BEST PART, SCOTTY! SHE FOUND HIS BOOK IN A USED BOOKSTORE!
BOOK? WHAT B-- OH! RIGHT! I FORGOT ABOUT THAT! WHAT WAS IT AGAIN? "HAMBURGER HELPER" OR --?
"HAMBURGER STEAK," BUT YOU KNEW THAT.
WOW, THAT'S AMAZING.
SEE?? MAYBE THIS WILL INSPIRE YOU TO FINALLY WRITE ANOTHER ONE!
SHH, MAN, THAT'S YOUR IN! YOU TELL HER SHE INSPIRED YOU TO FINALLY WRITE A NEW BOOK!
PANTHERS

SPEAKING OF LONG-AWAITED FOLLOW-UPS, HOW'S RITU FARING? SHE'S DUE ANY DAY, RIGHT?
YEP, END OF THE MONTH. I SHOULD REALLY MAKE AN EFFORT TO APPRECIATE THIS CALM BEFORE THE STORM.
IF THIS NEW ONE IS ANYTHING LIKE HER BROTHER WE'RE IN FOR A WORLD OF TROUBLE.

MISSY SAID THE SECOND ONE IS EASIER SINCE YOU HAVE SOME EXPERIENCE NOW. THE "ROUGH DRAFT" THEORY OF CHILD-REARING.
HOPEFULLY, BUT NOW WE HAVE THE ADDED LAYER OF HOW BRAIDEN WILL REACT TO A NEW BABY IN THE HOUSE.
WE TAKE IT FOR GRANTED THAT FAMILIES GROW AND CHANGE, BUT AS FAR AS HE KNOWS IT'S ALWAYS BEEN THE THREE OF US AND WOULD ALWAYS BE THE THREE OF US.

WE JUST HAVE TO HOPE FOR THE BEST, I SUPPOSE.
THE FOUR OF YOU IF YOU COUNT NINERA.
HAS HE SHOWN ANY SIGNS OF BEING JEALOUS YET?

WHY WOULD WE INCLUDE NINERA?

WELL, IF YOU THINK ABOUT IT, IT'S ALMOST AS IF HE HAS THREE PARENTS.

WHAT? HE DOESN'T. NINERA IS THE NANNY. HE KNOWS THAT.

BUT, I MEAN, LOOK AT IT FROM BRAIDEN'S POINT OF VIEW.

YOU GUYS I AM SO THIRSTY.
SHOULD WE STOP AT A BODEGA FOR MORE BEER?
WATER, MAYBE?

FOR AS LONG AS HE CAN REMEMBER THERE'S THIS THIRD ADULT WHO SPENDS THE DAY WITH HIM.

SHE'S THERE, WHAT? FIVE? SIX HOURS A DAY?

WHEN YOU WORK A FULL DAY AT SCHOOL YOU GET HOME AT FIVE OR SIXISH? HE PROBABLY GOES TO BED AROUND SEVEN, SO--

SO WHAT?? WHAT'S YOUR POINT??

WHOA, RELAX. I'M NOT MAKING ANY JUDGMENT, I'M JUST--

BRAIDEN KNOWS WE ARE HIS PARENTS.

HE UNDERSTANDS THAT RITU AND I ARE HIS PARENTS AND NINERA IS THE NANNY.

WE'RE THE ONES WHO BUST OUR ASSES TO FEED AND CLOTHE HIM AND PAY TO KEEP A ROOF OVER HIS HEAD.

WE'RE THE ONES WHO TOOK HIM TO THE E.R. AT 3 O'CLOCK IN THE MORNING, AND..
WAIT: YOU TOOK HIM TO THE EMERGENCY ROOM? IS HE OKAY?
"YEAH, YEAH, HE'S FINE NOW. HE JUST HAD A REALLY HIGH FEVER LAST WEEK. JUST ONE OF A THOUSAND TERRIFYING MOMENTS THAT COME WITH BEING A PARENT."
GREEN DAY
Get your chi
Vaccin
PENN STATE
SHIT.
YEAH, "SHIT."
SO IF EITHER OF YOU BROOMHEADS EVER HAS KIDS I'LL BE HAPPY TO TRADE NOTES, BUT UNTIL THEN KEEP YOUR OPINIONS ON MY PARENTING SKILLS TO YOURSELF.
I WASN'T..
OKAY.
MARCY... MARCY REALLY WANTS A KID. SOON.
YOU SHOULD. IT'S GREAT.

WE SHOULD, RIGHT?
I MEAN, I WANT TO BUT... I'M NOT SURE I'M READY. BUT, EVERYONE ALWAYS SAYS IT'S CHALLENGING BUT TOTALLY WORTH IT, RIGHT?
THAT REMINDS ME: DID YOU GUYS HEAR THAT THEY'RE DOING A NIGHTSTALKER REBOOT? UGH, WHAT A BAD IDEA.
GREEN DAY
SMOKE
DeGrassi

NO ONE EVER FEELS READY, AND THE PEOPLE WHO DO FEEL READY GET KNOCKED ON THEIR ASSES JUST THE SAME.
I JUST WANT OUR KIDS TO PLAY TOGETHER. YOU'RE DONE SKINNY-DIPPING, BILLY. TIME TO GROW UP.
HAHA, WELL, I HATE TO TELL YOU BUT MARCY AND I ARE GOING TO RAISE THEM NUDIST.
HA HA!

WHAT THE HELL ??
THIS ISN'T A BOX BALL COURT! IT'S --
I DON'T KNOW WHAT THIS IS!
HMM.

HOLD ON, HOLD ON! LET'S NOT GET ALL PANICKY. WE CAN FIGURE SOMETHING OUT.
DID MARCY E-MAIL BACK ABOUT THE FOUR OF US GETTING DINNER?
IF SHE DID RITU DIDN'T MENTION IT. DO YOU --
De Grassi
PANI
OKAY, OKAY, OKAY: BILLY, YOU GO IN BOX ONE.

SCOTTY STARTS IN BOX TWO AND I'LL START IN FOUR.
WE COULD JUST PLAY BASKETBALL INSTEAD.

"OKAY: BILLY SERVES THE BALL, BOUNCING IT INTO THE BOX IN FRONT OF ITHER OF US. LET'S UST SAY TO ME AS N EXAMPLE.
4
1
3
2
"SO THE BALL BOUNCES ONCE AND I HIT IT BACK --YOU CAN ONLY RETURN THE BALL TO THE SERVER."

WHERE DO YOU HIT IT? DIRECTLY TO ME OR DO YOU BOUNCE IT FIRST?
UM, EXCUSE ME?
HELLOO?

HI! UH... WHAT ARE YOU GUYS DOING OVER HERE?
HUH? OH, WE'RE JUST FIGURING OUT THIS GAME HE INVENTED.
I COULD FIGURE OUT A WAY TO ADD A FOURTH IF YOU'RE INTERESTED, HA.
I'M SEAN.

HAHA, WOW. NO, I WAS ASKING BECAUSE YOU CAN'T REALLY BE HERE.
UM... BUT WE'RE... IS SOMEONE USING THE COURT OR--?
YEAH, I MEAN, IF SOMEONE... WHAT DO YOU MEAN?

IF YOU READ THE SIGN ON THE GATE YOU'D KNOW THIS IS A CHILD-SAFE AREA.
NO ONE CAN BE HERE UNLESS THEY'RE A PARENT OR GUARDIAN TO A CHILD HERE.
OH.
OKAY, WE'RE SORRY. WE--
WAIT A MINUTE: WHAT??

BROWNIE.
HOW IS US PLAYING AN INCREDIBLE GAME I JUST INVENTED HURTING ANY--
DeGrassi

NO ONE IS INFERRING YOU'RE HURTING ANYONE. THIS IS A CHILD-SAFE PLAYGROUND WHERE KIDS CAN PLAY IN AN ENVIRONMENT THAT--

WHAT, YOU THINK WE'RE A ROAMING TRIO OF CHILD MOLESTERS??
HOKAY, LET'S--
WHAT I THINK DOESN'T MATTER. WHY DON'T WE ASK A COP WHAT HE OR SHE THINKS, HM?

A COP??
HA! OH YES! CHARGE US WITH INTENT TO USE A KICK BALL WITHIN TWENTY YARDS OF A--

OKAY, YOU KNOW WHAT? MISS, I APOLOGIZE. MY FRIEND AND I ARE GOING.

BROWNIE, BILLY AND I ARE LEAVING. YOU CAN STAY HERE AND PLAY YOUR GAME OR YOU CAN COME WITH US.
ALRIGHT, ALRIGHT--

JESUS, WHAT A BITCH!
AND TO THINK I WAS GOING TO IMAGINE HAVING SEX WITH HER LATER!
TRUST ME, YOU DON'T PLAY AROUND WHEN IT COMES TO THOSE PLAYGROUND NAZI-TYPES.
I JUST WANTED TO GET OUT BEFORE SHE SAW I HAD A BEER!
STILL..
IT'S KIND OF IRONIC I GO FOR THOSE MATERNAL HIPPIE GIRLS, ISN'T IT?
HA! IT MAKES PERFECT SENSE TO ME.
SO WHAT DO YOU GUYS WANNA DO? GO BACK AND SEE IF THE BASKETBALL GUYS ARE DONE?
MMM... I DUNNO. IT'S GETTING KIND OF LATE. I THINK I'M GONNA SPLIT.
AWW, BOO!
NEXT TIME WE'LL HAVE BROWNIE GO AN HOUR EARLY TO RESERVE THE COURT.
TXT FROM DENISE: r u around? =)

BOY, SCOTTY REALLY GOT PISSED WHEN I BROUGHT UP THAT NANNY STUFF.
YEAH, I THINK EVERY PARENT IS AFRAID THEY AREN'T DOING A GOOD ENOUGH JOB.
I WISH WE COULD AFFORD A NANNY.
PSSH! THAT ISN'T TRUE. HAVE YOU SEEN SOME OF THESE SO-CALLED "PARENTS?"

I WAS ON THE TRAIN AT 11:30 THE OTHER NIGHT AND THERE WAS THIS SLACK-JAWED MOM GIVING HER BRATS SODA TO KEEP THEM QUIET.
LMFA

SODA! AT 11:30 AT NIGHT! THEN I BET WHEN THEY GOT HOME SHE SMACKED THEM FOR MAKING TOO MUCH NOISE.
BUT EVEN YOU HAVE TO ADMIT THE NANNY THING IS A LITTLE WEIRD:
"OH! WE WERE BLESSED WITH THIS ADORABLE CHILD WE LOVE SO MUCH AND WOULD DO ANYTHING FOR!"
"I KNOW: LET'S LEAVE HER IN THE CARE OF AN ECUADORIAN WOMAN WITH A THIRD-GRADE EDUCATION!"
NAILS
DeGrassi

IT'S A GREAT WAY FOR A KID TO LEARN SPANISH, I HEAR.

HA, THAT'S TRUE.

ALTHOUGH IF THAT'S YOUR THINKING YOU SHOULD GO WITH A CHINESE NANNY.

BY THE TIME YOUR KID GROWS UP THEY WILL OWN THIS PLACE.

SO...

SO YOU AND MARCY ARE REALLY DOING THIS, HUH?

IT SEEMS THAT WAY. WE CAN'T PUT IT OFF FOREVER, RIGHT?

I JUST HAVE A HARD TIME WRAP-PING MY HEAD AROUND THE WHOLE FATHER IDEA.

BY THE TIME MY DAD WAS MY AGE I WAS, LIKE, THIRTEEN YEARS OLD.

CAN YOU IMAGINE ME TAKING CARE OF A THIRTEEN YEAR-OLD?

"OH... RIGHT."

BUT THAT WAS LIKE A THOUSAND YEARS AGO! YOU WERE YOUNG AND VIRILE AND IN COLLEGE!
SINCE THEN YOUR BOYS HAVE BEEN SUBJECTED TO YEARS OF CELL PHONE RADIATION AND TIGHT UNDERPANTS.
YOU SHOULD GET TESTED.
DeGrassi

GOD, THAT WAS SEVENTEEN YEARS AGO.
THAT KID WOULD'VE BEEN OLD ENOUGH TO DRIVE.

UM... SO DO YOU KNOW WHAT SHE'S UP TO THESE DAYS?
CARRIE?

WE WERE FACEBOOK FRIENDS FOR A FEW YEARS, BUT THEN I GOT ALL PARANOID MARCY WOULD NOTICE AND GET MAD, SO I UNFRIENDED HER. SHE DIDN'T UPDATE MUCH BUT..
SUZANNE VEGA!!

"LUKA" IS BY SUZANNE VEGA, NOT AIMEE MANN!
BEFORE YOU WERE SAYING--
HAHA!
I WAS SHOCKED YOU LET THAT ONE PAST YOU BEFORE!

THAT IS WEIRD. I GUESS YEARS OF MARIJUANA ABUSE HAVE TAKEN A TOLL ON, UH, ON MY... YOU KNOW, UH...
DON'T TELL ME! I'LL GET IT! HAHA!
HAHA, OKAY, SHOOT ME AN E-MAIL WHEN YOU GET IT.
SEE YOU NEXT TIME, CHAMP.
DeGrassi
PANTHERS

TXT FROM BILLY: MEET AT PERRO'S FOR DINNER?
US
YOU WANNA GO MEET DADDY FOR DINNER?
LET'S GO!

C'MON, FROGGY, ONE MORE BITE...
NNN!!
COOKIES
TXT FROM SCOTTY: STILL OUT WITH GUYS. WILL UPDATE.
RASNGET!!
OKAY, ONE MORE AND THEN BATH TIME...

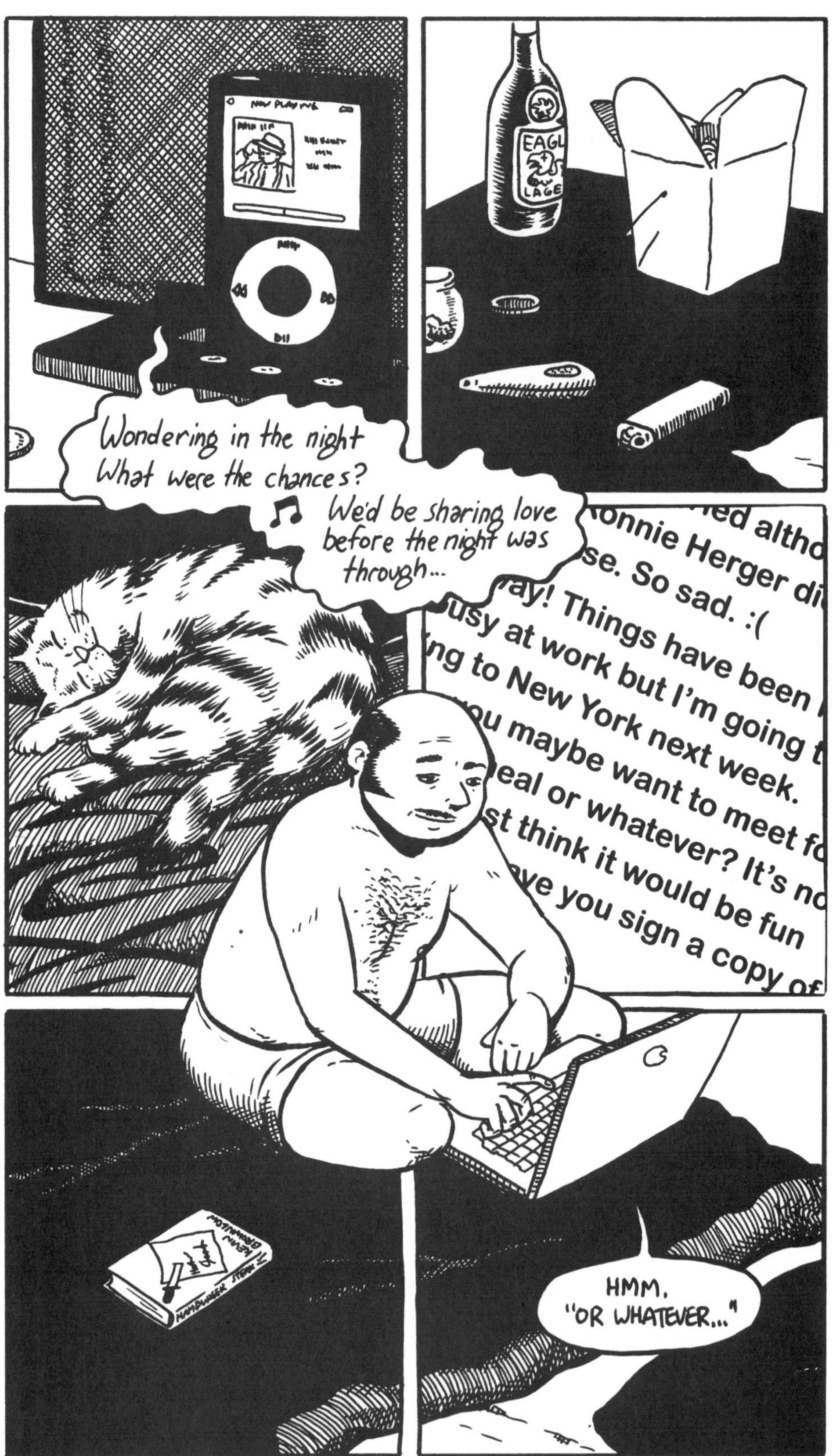
Wondering in the night
What were the chances?
♫ We'd be sharing love before the night was through...
nnie Herger di
se. So sad. :(
ay! Things have been
usy at work but I'm going t
ng to New York next week.
ou maybe want to meet fo
eal or whatever? It's no
st think it would be fun
ave you sign a copy of
HMM.
"OR WHATEVER..."

HEY, BILLY.

WHY ARE YOU ON POOP PATROL?

WHERE'S LUIS?

:Sigh:

HE HAD TO GO HOME EARLY.

WHAT CAN I DO FOR YOU, DANIELLA?

AND PLEASE DON'T SAY GIVE YOU FRIDAY OFF.

BUT IT'S DOG DAYS! THE BIG SUMMER CRUNCH!
OH, MAN. WHAT'S THIS BETTER JOB?
I GOT A JOB AT THE H&M IN UNION SQUARE!
I GOTTA MOVE ON. I DON'T WANNA BE PICKING UP DOG SHIT THE REST OF MY LIFE!
(NO OFFENSE OR WHATEVER)

NO, I'M SORRY, YOU'RE RIGHT. CONGRATULATIONS.
CAN YOU AT LEAST--
UH, BILLY?

SHE'S HERE.

I DON'T UNDERSTAND. YOU SAY ANOTHER DOG BIT HER? IS SHE OKAY?
ARE YOU OKAY, HONEY?
NO, NO, SHE'S FINE. SHE WAS THE ONE WHO BIT ANOTHER DOG.
THE OTHER DOG--

ELLIE?? BUT THAT'S IMPOSSIBLE!
SHE'S NEVER SO MUCH AS BARKED AT ANOTHER DOG! IT MUST'VE BEEN SOMEONE ELSE.
YIP! YIP! YIP!

I'M SORRY, MISS, BUT ONE OF OUR CAMP COUNSELORS SAW IT AND HE DEF--
FIRST OFF, "SIR", I'M NOT ADMITTING TO ANY OF THIS. I THINK YOUR EMPLOYEE IS EITHER A) WRONG, OR B) A LIAR! SECOND, THEY..
YIP! YIP! YIP!

WHY WOU
LIE? WHAT
MOTIVE FO
SECONDLY, THEY'RE DOGS! THIS MUST HAPPEN ALL THE TIME!!
YIP! YIP!

WELL, I'M AFRAID IN THIS CASE IT WAS SERIOUS ENOUGH THAT ELLIE IS NO LONGER WELCOME AT RAISE THE WOOF.

"NO LONGER WELCOME?" "NO LONGER--?!" WHAT DOES THAT EVEN MEAN? I'VE BEEN--
YIP
YIP! YI
EANS Y
OTHER PL
BOARD HE
YOU'RE KICKING HER OUT? OVER SOME STUPID LITTLE BITE?! THIS IS RIDICULOUS, YOU KNOW THAT, RIGHT? I'VE BEEN--
CAN YOU PLEASE LOWER--

OKAY, YOU KNOW WHAT?
NORMALLY, I'M A VERY KIND, EASY-GOING PERSON WHO WOULD NOT MAKE A BIG DEAL ABOUT THINGS BUT I WANT THE MANAGER, OKAY?
WE'VE BEEN COMING HERE FOR SEVEN MO
AND HAVE--
OKAY, WELL, YOU KNOW WHAT? I'M THE MANAGER AND I'M TELLING--
OH! HA HA. YOU TOTALLY GOT ME. THE OWNER THEN AND DON'T--
THE OWNER STEPPED OUT FOR A MOMENT BUT SHE SHOULD BE BACK FROM FLORIDA IN THREE MONTHS.
IF YOU WANT TO WAIT.
OKAY.
YOU KNOW WHAT? YOU JUST LOST A CUSTOMER.
AND JUST BECAUSE YOU HATE YOUR SHITTY JOB AND STUPID LIFE IS NO REASON TO TREAT PEOPLE LIKE GARBAGE.
I'M SORRY YOUR BAND DIDN'T MAKE IT OR YOUR SNOWBOARDING CAREER FIZZLED BUT DON'T TAKE IT OUT ON US.

COME ON, ELLIE-HONEY.
THOOM
POKE!
WHO LET THE DOGS OUT?? WHO...

HELLO? MOM?
OUTTA THE ROAD, FUCK·HOLE!!
SH I T!
GLOOP
CRACK!
LADIES AND ≡CRACKLE≡ BECAUSE OF A SICK PASSENGER AT BERGEN STREET ≡CRACKLE≡ HELD MOMENTAR
THIS LITTLE HEART OF MINE I'M GONNA LET IT SHINE!!
≡COUGH≡

SNURFLE
Wheeze!

HEY! I HOPE YOU MANAGED TO AVOID THE RAIN.

I HAVE HAD A DAY. I KNOW I'M SUPPOSED TO COOK BUT CAN WE ORDER IN?
OHHH, MY POOR, MOIST HERO. DOES MEXICAN WORK?
OH, AND YOU HAVE SOME VOICEMAILS.

UH-OH. PLEASE SAY IT'S SOME GOOD NEWS.
DUNNO

BEEP
NARY
HEY, MAN, IT'S ME. I GOT AN UPDATE ON MY HIGH SCHOOL GIRL. GIMME A CALL. MAYBE GET SOME LUNCH?
BEEP
HI, BILLY! HI, MARCY, IT'S MOM CALLING!

I'M TRYING TO-(WHAT DOES THIS SAY? "EXIT?")

:Sigh: I'M TRYING TO FIGURE OUT HOW TO PROGRAM THIS NEW DVD TO RECORD "ANIMAL HOARDERS" BUT IT KEEPS--

("DO YOU WISH TO RECORD THIS PROGRAM?" YES!)

--BUT WHEN I DO IT FILLS UP THE WHOLE DARN THING WITH SHOWS. HOW DO I--

("ARE YOU SURE YOU WANT TO DELETE--" NO! I DON'T WANT--

MY GOD! OKAY, NEXT TIME YOU GUYS COME OVER YOU'RE GOING TO HAVE TO SHOW YOUR FATHER HOW TO PROGRAM THIS THING BECAUSE I AM AT WITS' END!

OKAY, LOVE YOU GUYS!

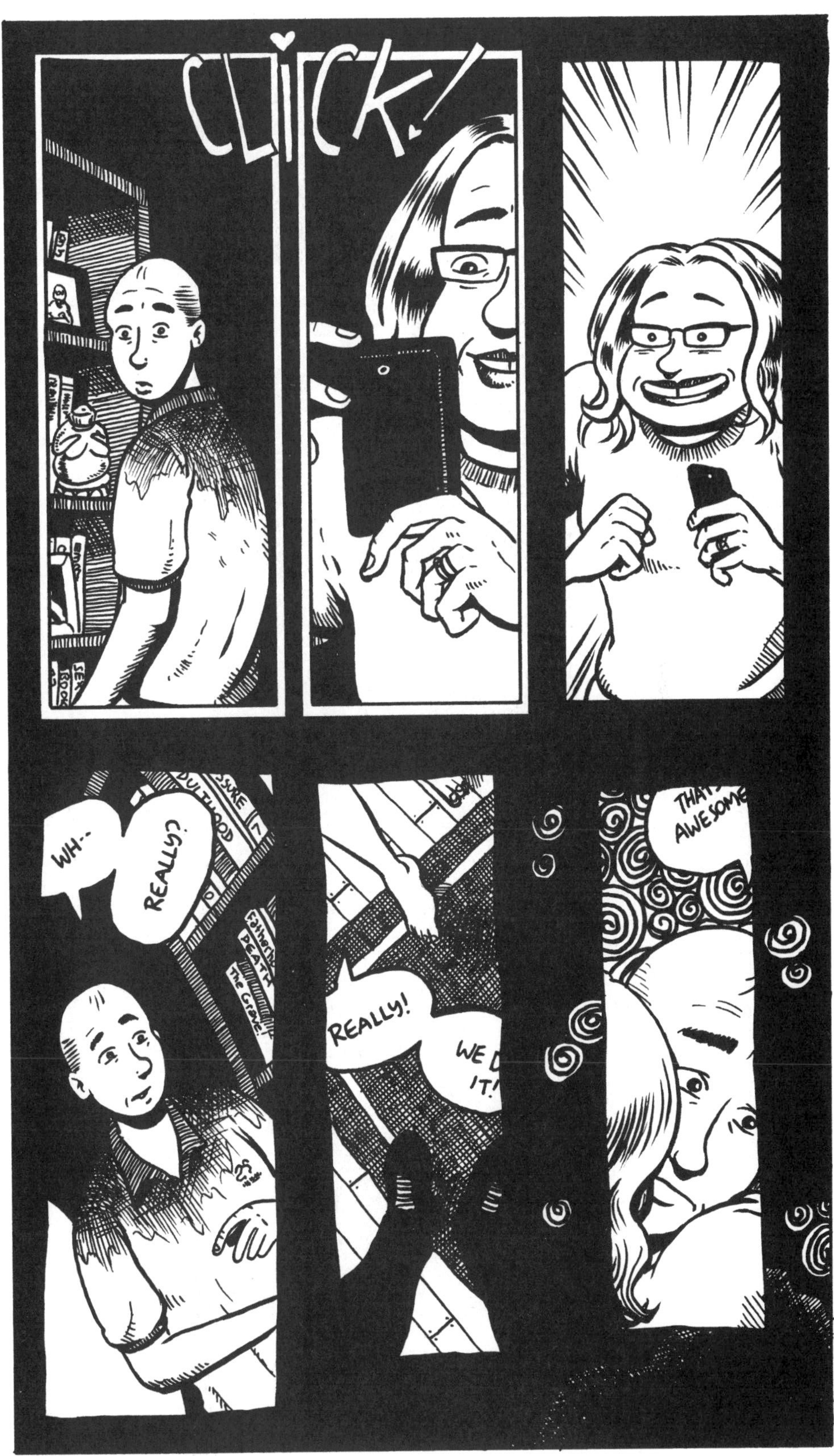
CLICK!
WH--
REALLY?
REALLY!
WE D
IT!
THAT'
AWESOM

ONE OF THE ENDURING MYSTERIES OF SCIENCE IS THE ORIGIN OF LIFE ON EARTH.
DID IT START AROUND HYDROTHERMAL VENTS AT THE BOTTOM OF THE OCEAN?
MAYBE A COMBINATION OF CHEMICALS AND ELECTRICITY IN A SHALLOW TIDE POOL?
ONE INTRIGUING THEORY IS THAT LIFE CAME TO EARTH IN THE FORM OF MICROBES LIVING ON ASTEROIDS,
MAKING US ALL DESCENDANTS OF ALIEN ASTRONAUTS!

SO, I FIGURE MEET A GIRL YOU KNOW ONLINE YOU H WON'T BE AS ATTRA HER PROFILE PIC
LET'S SA 20% BETT LOOKING TH DOES IN REAL
YOU HAVE TO ASSUME SHE'S USING THE MOST FLA PICTURE SHE CAN GET AWAY WITH -- PROBABLY A FEW YEARS OLD, PROBABLY A FEW POUNDS LIGHTER, ETC.

SHE CAN'T GO MORE THAN 20% OR THE GUY WILL GET STICKER SHOCK WHEN THEY FINALLY MEET.
SO I'M WAITING, FIGURING SHE'LL BE AT LEAST 80% AS GOOD-LOOKING AS THE PICTURE SHE SENT. WHICH I WOULD BE FINE WITH!
"IS THIS EVEN THE SAME GIRL I'VE BEEN BEATING OFF TO IMAGINING HOW THIS DATE WILL GO?"
JAKE! HELP! THE PUMPKIN WITCH GOT ME!
OKAY, SO THE GOOD NEWS IS THAT SHE SHOWS UP AND I'M NOT DISAPPOINTED.
GRANTED, SHE'S NOW A MIDDLE-AGED WOMAN FROM PHILLY AND NOT THE SOPHOMORE FROM ENGLISH CLASS.
BUT! I CAN SEE JUST ENOUGH OF TH GIRL TO, YOU KNOW "CLICK."
OH! AND YOU'LL BE PLEASED TO KNOW I WENT AU NATURALE..
FULL-BLOWN HATLESS!
HANG ON, BUDDY!
ZZAPP!
GOT HER!!

SO WE'RE HANGING OUT AT THE BAR, WHICH THANKFULLY ISN'T TOO PACKED, AND IT'S JUST SO FUCKING WEIRD. IT'S LIKE A ROGER RABBIT THING, YOU KNOW?
WORLDS ARE COLLIDING! IT'S IMPOSSIBLE AND YET HERE SHE IS.
SO WE'RE CHATTING, AND SHE'S TELLING ME ALL ABOUT PEOPLE WE WENT TO HIGH SCHOOL WITH: DID I HEAR ABOUT ANDY WICKS? SAM WEIR HAS TWO BOYS (AGES SEVEN AND FOUR). TAMMY LITTLENUT MOVED TO WOODLAWN. BLAH BLAH BLAH.
CRAB PRINCESS! USE THE ROPE AND PULL US UP!
my GLOB!
ISN'T BEING THAT FRIENDLY WITH PEOPLE YOU KNEW IN HIGH SCHOOL KIND OF A CRY FOR HELP?
(OKAY, BEFORE YOU SAY ANYTHING, THE ANSWER IS YES. YES IT IS.)
SKULL
OKAY, SO WE'RE CHATTING, WE'RE DRINKING AND SHE'S ASKING A LOT OF STUFF ABOUT ME-- DID I REGRET GETTING DIVORCED? HOW COOL IS IT TO BE A REAL WRITER?--
BUT WHEN I ASK ABOUT HER, SHE'S KIND OF VAGUE AND EVASIVE. ANOTHER WARNING SIGN.

IF YOU'LL RECALL, SHE ORIGINALLY TOLD ME THAT SHE WAS DIVORCED.
THREE FROZEN COSMOS LATER, THIS TURNS OUT TO NOT BE THE CASE.
THE CASE, AS IT TURNS OUT, IS THAT SHE IS MERELY SEPARATED.
I WAS SURPRISED TO FIND MYSELF KIND OF RELIEVED AT THIS. IT SORT OF TAKES THE, UH, PRESSURE OFF.
YOU KNOW, ANY RELATIONSHIP PRESSURE, YOU KNOW?
SKULL
SO, WE'RE CHATTING AND DRINKING MORE, AND SUDDENLY, I'M GETTING THIS VIBE, YOU KNOW? LIKE, THIS GIRL MIGHT ACTUALLY BE, LIKE, INTO ME!
UH... MARCY IS PREGNANT.
WITH A BABY.

WOW. WHAT ARE YOU GONNA DO?
OH, WAIT! I MEAN CONGRATS, MAN.
ARE YOU..? CAN I..?
OH, SURE. THANKS.
HOW ARE WE GONNA GET OUTTA THIS, FINN?
IT'S WEIRD, CUZ WE'VE OBVIOUSLY BEEN TALKING ABOUT IT FOR AWHILE BUT NOW... NOW IT'S LIKE IT'S REAL, RIGHT?
GURGLEGURGLEGURGLEGURGLEGURGUR
IT'S NOT "LIKE" REAL, IT IS REAL!
HAHA
PHOOOO
YEAH, IT'S LIKE YOU'RE AT THAT MOMENT WHEN THEY PUT THE SAFETY BAR DOWN ON THE ROLLY COASTER.
YOU'RE ALL LOCKED IN AND SHIT AND ALL OF A SUDDEN YOU'RE ALL, LIKE:
CHINGACHINGACHINGACHING HA HA!
HA HA.
YEAH.
SKULL

I HAVE TO ADMIT I FEEL KIND OF FREAKED OUT SINCE SHE TOLD ME. I STILL DON'T FEEL READY.
AT LEAST YOU HAVE SCOTTY AND RITU TO HELP YOU GUYS OUT. THEY'RE HAVING NUMBER TWO ANY MINUTE.
THEY MUST'VE BEEN EXCITED WHEN YOU TOLD THEM.
SKULL
NO, WE ACTUALLY HAVEN'T TOLD ANYONE YET. SHE'S ONLY A MONTH IN AND DOESN'T WANT TO, YOU KNOW, JINX IT.
ONLY A MONTH? SO THERE'S STILL-- IT'S STILL EARLY GOING. YOU'LL HAVE TIME TO ADJUST.
BUT... WHAT IS IT YOU'RE WORRIED ABOUT? MONEY? CHOPS?
AH, YOU KNOW, MONEY, AM I--
WAIT, WHAT ABOUT CHOPS?
SKULL

I DON'T KNOW, DO DOGS LIKE BABIES? OR DO THEY TRY TO SUFFOCATE THEM LIKE CATS DO?
WHAT?? NO! THEY..
WHAT, ARE YOU TRYING TO COME UP WITH SHIT FOR ME TO WORRY ABOUT??
HAHA! NO!
DUDE, THE ONLY THING I KNOW LESS ABOUT THAN BABIES IS DOGS,
BUT THIS IS GOOD! WE'RE WORKING THROUGH IT. WE CAN CROSS YOUR DOG EATING YOUR BABY OFF YOUR WORRY LIST. WHAT ELSE?
MONEY? HOW TO PAY FOR COLLEGE?
HAVING TO GET A BIGGER PLACE?
LOSING HER AT THE MALL?
KIDNAPPERS
YOUR AWKWARD FEELINGS WHEN YOU DRIVE THE BABY-SITTER HOME?
BEING A POSITIVE MALE INFLUENCE FOR YOUR SON?
HAVING TO BE FRIENDLY TO YOUR KID'S FRIEND'S BORING PARENTS?
I HATE TO TELL YOU, BUT TO HER YOU'RE JUST SOME OLD, WRINKLED DAD.

SERIOUSLY? I THOUGHT SHE KINDA LIKED MY "CLASSIC ROCK" MIX.
SORRY, MY BROTHER, SHE WAS JUST BEING POLITE.
YOU DON'T NEED TO WORRY. HAVE YOU SEEN SOME OF THESE BREEDERS? IF THOSE SLACK-JAWED YOKELS CAN DO IT, YOU GUYS CAN.
YOU WENT TO COLLEGE AND SHIT!
I GUESS SO, BUT...
I'M HAPPY WITH THINGS HOW THEY ARE.
OF COURSE YOU ARE: YOU'RE STONED.
TRUST ME, A YEAR FROM NOW YOU'LL BE ONE OF THOSE DADS TELLING ME THAT MY LIFE ISN'T COMPLETE UNTIL I'VE SEEN MY CHILD LOOK AT ME AND SMILE BECAUSE HE JUST SHIT HIS DRAWERS AGAIN.
SKULL
THANKS FOR TALKING ME DOWN.
AND... I DIDN'T WANT TO BRING IT UP, BUT YOU REALLY SHOULD HAVE A KID.
MY LIFE IS ALREADY FULFILLED IN WAYS I DARED NOT IMAGINE.
DON'T SAY THAT UNTIL YOU'VE PLAYED "DARK CENTAUR 2" ON THE X-BOX.

YOU, UH... WANT I SHOULD FIRE HER UP?
UM... I DON'T KNOW...
TXT TO MARCY: RUNNING LATE. HOME SOON! XO
SKULL
SKULL
HEY, YOU WANNA GET LUNCH ON TUESDAY? YOU CAN TAKE ME OUT FOR MY BIRTHDAY.
VIDEO2
JEEZ, YOUR BIRTHDAY AGAIN? WHAT IS IT, THE BIG FOUR-OH?
JUST THE BIG THREE-EIGHT.
THE MEDIUM SIZED THREE-EIGHT.
SKULL
OKAY, READY?
exhale SOCK IT TO ME.
SKULL

WHOA. THAT WAS... AMAZING.
THE PART WHERE THAT SPIKED THING CRUSHED THE--
OH! SHIT, I GOTTA RUN.
SKULL
10:30
3 missed alerts
OKAY, SO: LUNCH?
SURE.
AND, UH, CONGRATULATIONS, AGAIN ON THE WHOLE, AH, BABY THING.
SKULL
THANKS, MAN.
CLUNK

OW.

TA-DA!
PLAYING HOUSE
HOLY SHIT, THAT'S CREEPY!
HAHA! HE GOT YOU THIS FOR YOUR BIRTHDAY?
YEAH, WE SAW HIM AT FUNCLES.
"HEDDO, TCODDY..." WAIT. "HEDDO SHCODDY! NY NANE ID KEDDY!"

ORIGINALLY I WAS KEEPING HIM ON THE DRESSER BUT MARCY WOKE UP IN THE MIDDLE OF THE NIGHT AND FREAKED OUT.

ERF

HEH, CAN YOU BLAME HER?

SO NOW HE STAYS IN THE CLOSET.

HOW DID BROWNIE TAKE THE NEWS ABOUT THE BABY?

ASSUMING YOU TOLD HIM.

THE CHICKEN WAS DELICIOUS, MARCE. GOOD CALL!
YEAH, WE DON'T HAVE ANY THAI PLACES IN OUR NEIGHBORHOOD. AT LEAST NOT YET.
AH, THE SACRIFICES ONE MAKES BEING A PART OF THE FIRST WAVE OF GENTRIFICATION!
ANYBODY WANT A BEER WHILE I'M UP? SCOTTY?

UMMM...?
GO AHEAD.

IIIIII... THINK I'LL PASS.
EARLY DAY.
AWW, WUSS.
MARCE? BREWSKI?

I THINK I'LL PASS, TOO.
DON'T WORRY: WHEN YOU HIT THE THIRD TRIMESTER YOU'RE ALLOWED A GLASS OF WINE!
WHAT WAS THE STORY YOU WERE GOING TO TELL ME?
ABOUT GINA?

YES!
I THINK SHE'S GETTING SERIOUS WITH SOME GUY! I HAVEN'T TALKED TO HER BUT SHE'S BEEN POSTING SOME ENIGMATIC STUFF ON FACEBOOK.
SOMETHING'S UP I TELLS YA.
OOH! "ENIGMATIC" HOW??
I'M SORRY, WHO'S GINA AGAIN?
BOOBS.
OH! RIGHT!
GO ON.
"ENIGMATIC" HOW?
WHAT, I TOOK THE QUICKEST ROUTE! YOU KNEW EXACTLY WHAT I MEANT.
UM..., JUST A LOT OF, LIKE, HIPPIE, LOVEY-DOVEY STUFF ABOUT THE UNIVERSE PROVIDING.

WELL, GOOD FOR HER. I HOPE HE'S BETTER THAN THE ASSHOLE.
SHE DESERVES A DECENT GUY AFTER ALL SHE'S BEEN THROUGH.
OH, THIS IS THE ONE WITH THE--?
MAN.
LOOK, I'M SORRY TO BE THE ONE TO SAY IT BUT IF YOU MAKE IT TO AGE...35? AND YOU'VE NEVER BEEN IN A SERIOUS RELATIONSHIP?
IT'S BECAUSE YOU DON'T WANT TO BE IN A RELATIONSHIP.
BUT, SCOTTY, SHE DOES WANT TO BE IN A RELATIONSHIP! DESPERATELY!
A HUSBAND! KIDS! IT'S ALL SHE TALKS ABOUT!
JESUS, HOW AM I GOING TO TELL HER WE'RE PREGNANT??
FINE, SHE TALKS ABOUT IT, BUT ON SOME LEVEL SHE DOESN'T THINK SHE REALLY DESERVES ALL THAT.

WHAT?? A SECOND AGO YOU WERE DESCRIBING HER AS "BOOBS" BUT NOW YOU'VE GOT HER ALL FIGURED OUT?
AND SHE COMPLETELY PUTS HERSELF OUT THERE: SPEED DATING, INTERNET DATING, SINGLES, UH, UH, MIXERS!
LOOK, THERE'S PLENTY OF DECENT GUYS OUT THERE. NOT RICH, WITTY HUNKS -- DECENT GUYS.
BUT SOMEHOW THE CLOSEST SHE'S COME TO ATTAINING THIS DREAM SHE'S SO DESPERATE FOR IS DATING A GUY FOR FOUR MONTHS -- WHO HIT HER?
THAT'S NOT BAD LUCK: THAT'S PSYCHOLOGY.
UH, TECHNICALLY SHE DATED ONE GUY FOR SEVEN MONTHS.
BUT HE WAS MARRIED, SO...
OH! THAT REMINDS ME: BROWNIE WENT OUT WITH HIS HIGH SCHOOL GIRL!

SPEAKING OF FOREVER ALONE...
DID HE ATTAIN HIS LIFELONG DREAM? —HOW DID IT GO?
UM, GOOD-- I THINK. HE STARTED TELLING ME THE STORY AND WE GOT SIDETRACKED BUT I THINK IT WENT WELL.
I KNOW HE SAYS HE NEVER WANTS TO GET MARRIED AGAIN BUT I THINK, SECRETLY, HE'S, YOU KNOW, KIND OF LONELY.
WHAT?? DIDN'T HE MAKE THAT BIG PROCLAMATION THAT ALL HE NEEDED WAS INTERNET PORN AND WEED?
OOH! MAYBE WE CAN HOOK HIM UP WITH GINA!
HA HAHA!
HE DID ONCE ADMIT TO ME THAT A BIG REASON HE MARRIED LISA WAS TO BE A PART OF "THE GANG."
PART OF OUR GANG.

AWW, NOW I FEEL BAD.
PSSH! IF YOU'RE GOING TO FEEL BAD FOR ANYONE IT SHOULD BE LISA. THEY WERE MARRIED FOR WHAT? THREE YEARS?
WELL, IT'S NOT LIKE SHE WAS SUCH A PRIZE. UGH, SHE WAS A DRIP.
GOD, THAT'S TRUE. I RESENTED THAT WHEN WE'D HANG OUT HE WOULD JUST DUMP HER ON MARCE AND I.
HE'D BE LECTURING YOU GUYS ABOUT A MOVIE OR ONE OF HIS CRACKPOT THEORIES AND WE'D BE STUCK TRYING TO MAKE CONVERSATION WITH MISS DISHWATER.
HEHHEH SEE, THAT'S WHY I THOUGHT THEY WERE A GOOD PAIRING, ACTUALLY.
SINCE SHE HAD NO PERSONALITY SHE WAS A GOOD COUNTERPOINT TO HIS, UH, YOU KNOW, DOMINEERING PERSONALITY.
I DON'T KNOW IF HE WANTS A PARTNER SO MUCH AS AN AUDIENCE.

UM, YEAH, WE HAVEN'T DISCUSSED IT, REALLY. YET.

I GUESS OUR PARENTS WILL HELP OUT, RIGHT?

BILLY, YOUR PARENTS LIVE IN WESTCHESTER, RIGHT? ISN'T THAT ABOUT TWO HOURS AWAY?

YEAH, IN ROCKLAND, ACTUALLY, BUT, I MEAN, THEY'LL WANT TO HELP.

IT'LL BE THEIR GRAND-CHILD, RIGHT?

THEIR FIRST GRANDCHILD, SO...

THAT IS TRUE, BUT ARE THEY GOING TO COME DOWN EVERY DAY? THAT'S QUITE A COMMUTE.

THAT'S TRUE. THEY...

UM. I DON'T KNOW, MAYBE A NANNY'S THE ANSWER, RIGHT?
SHIT, RITU, THEY SAID THEY HAVEN'T HAD A CHANCE TO DISCUSS IT YET, OKAY? LIGHTEN UP!
WHAT, I WAS JUST ASKING. I WASN'T BEING--
DON'T WORRY, YOU GUYS WILL FIGURE IT OUT. IF NOT, RITU WILL BE GLAD TO HELP YOU DECIDE.
WHEN WE HIRED NINERA I DIDN'T HAVE TO DO ANYTHING. ONE DAY SHE SHOWED UP FOR WORK AND I WAS LIKE "OH! GREAT! PLEASED TO MEET YOU!"
THAT'S NOT TRUE. YOU KNOW I TRIED TO INCLUDE YOU IN THE PROCESS, BUT YOU DIDN'T SHOW MUCH OF AN INTEREST, AND SOME-ONE HAD TO MAKE A DECISION.
I WAS INTERESTED, BUT YOU NEVER LET--
YOU KNOW WHAT? FORGET IT.
HMMF YES. EXACTLY.
OKAY, JUST BECAUSE I DON'T WANT TO ARGUE IN FRONT OF OUR FRIENDS DOESN'T MEAN YOU-- THAT DOESN'T MEAN YOU SOMEHOW PROVED YOUR POINT, OKAY??

SO, YOU'RE FREE TO COMPLAIN ABOUT ME IN FRONT OF THEM BUT IF I DEFEND MYSELF THEN I'M THE ONE BEING..

I WASN'T "COMPLAINING" ABOUT YOU I WAS JUST POINTING OUT THAT YOU HAVE A WAY OF MAKING PEOPLE--

HEY! WHO'S UP FOR SOME MEGA-UNO?
SEVEN DECKS OF FUN! HA HA!
UNO

REVERSE.
BLUE EIGHT.
OH, MY TURN? RED EIGHT.
DRAW TWO.

I STILL HAVE TO TAKE CHOPSY OUT FOR HIS NIGHT W-A-L-K.
!
I DON'T REMEMBER RITU AND SCOTTY BEING THAT BICKERY BEFORE. WAS IT JUST ME OR WAS IT, LIKE, SUPER AWKWARD?
NO, IT WAS KIND OF WEIRD.
I THINK SCOTTY'S BEEN CRUNCHED AT WORK, AND WITH THE NEW BABY COMING... I GUESS THEY'RE PROBABLY STRESSED.
RIGHT? RIGHT, FART MONKEY? RRRAR!!
SNORT
OHH! DON'T USE YOUR HAND AS A TOY...
YOU'RE RIGHT, YOU'RE RIGHT.
Sigh
OKAY, LET ME TAKE HIM OUT BEFORE I FALL ASLEEP.
ERF

RITU'S RIGHT, THOUGH. WE'VE GOT TO FIGURE OUT SOME WAY TO HANDLE THE BABY WITH BOTH OF US WORKING.
"THE BABY."
IT STILL SOUNDS... STRANGE.
HOW LONG WILL IT TAKE US TO GET USED TO SAYING THAT?
"DID YOU FEED THE BABY YET?"
"OH MY GOD! WE FORGOT THE BABY!"
HeeHee, I KNOW.
IT REMINDS ME OF WHEN WE FIRST GOT MARRIED. I WAS SO SELF-CONSCIOUS ABOUT REFERRING TO YOU AS "MY HUSBAND."
I FELT LIKE A LITTLE KID PLAYING HOUSE.
TOTALLY.
I GUESS I ALWAYS THOUGHT THAT BY THE TIME I HAD A KID I WOULD BE...
I DON'T KNOW, THAT I WOULD FEEL MORE GROWN UP.
IS THAT WEIRD?

IT'S NATURAL TO BE NERVOUS. I AM, TOO. WE'LL FIGURE IT OUT, LAMBCHOP.
BESIDES, WHAT WILL MAKE YOU FEEL MORE LIKE A GROWN-UP THAN CHANGING YOUR DAUGHTER'S POOPY DIAPER?
OH NO YOU DON'T! DIAPERS ARE LADY WORK. I'M IN CHARGE OF STUFF LIKE TEACHING HER TO THROW A FOOT-BALL AND CHANGE A TIRE.
SNORT!
SCRATCH!
SCRITCH!

HA! I WOULD GO ALONG WITH THAT IF I THOUGHT YOU COULD EVEN IDENTIFY A FOOTBALL.
HAR DE HAR HAR.
OKAY, SEE YOU IN A BIT.

Dark Energy
HMM. FUNNY, I HADN'T HEARD THAT.
OH, SURE, SURE.'
THEY SAY THE ABILITY TO RECOGNIZE THE HUMAN FACE IS HARD-WIRED INTO A BABY'S BRAIN.
YEAH, I SAW THIS TRIPPY THING ABOUT IT OVER ON THAT SCIENCE CHANNEL.
WOW.

LIKE THAT ELECTRICAL BOX-THINGIE. PRETTY MUCH ANY TIME YOU PUT TWO DOTS ABOVE A LINE, BLAMMO: YOU'LL SEE A FACE.

HA, YES, I SUPPOSE THAT IS TRUE.

LIKE... CARS...
IT MAKES SENSE, RIGHT? AS A SURVIVAL THING? ABOVE ALL ELSE A BABY HAS TO GET AN ADULT TO BOND WITH IT OR IT WILL LITERALLY DIE.
THAT MEANS EYE-CONTACT AND SMILES...

YEP.

I'D ALWAYS HEARD THAT HORMONES FLOOD A NEW MOTHER'S BODY TO ENCOURAGE THAT BONDING. I WONDER HOW ADOPTIVE MOTHERS WORK THAT, Y'KNOW?
CAN YOU "TRICK" YOUR BODY INTO MAKING THE HORMONES? CAN YOU GET A SHOT OR SOMETHING?

WE USED TO BE FRIENDS, RIGHT?

:Sigh: WELL, I COULDN'T FIND ANY VASES OR ANYTHING SO I GUESS I'LL JUST BRING THEM HOME WITH ME.
JEEZ, I'M SORRY FOR THE HASSLE, SCOTTY. YOU WOULD ASSUME THEY WOULD HAVE VASES FOR THE PATIENTS.
I MEAN, IT'S A HOSPITAL, RIGHT? PEOPLE GET SENT FLOWERS ALL THE TIME SO WHY WOULDN'T..

HOW'S OUR LITTLE HOMUNCULUS?
MM, GOOD. THE NURSE STOPPED IN. I THINK WE'RE A LITTLE TIRED.
SEAN'S JUST BEEN TELLING ME ABOUT DEAD BABIES.
?! NO, I WASN'T! ALIVE! ALIVE BABIES!
THEY'RE ALIVE BECAUSE THEY BOND WITH ADULTS! I SAW IT IN THIS DOCU-MENTARY ONE TIME!

IT'S PRETTY AMAZING, REALLY. WE START OFF SO TINY AND BLOBBY AND HELPLESS-- ESPECIALLY COMPARED TO OTHER MAMMALS. WE'RE ALMOST LIKE BABY KANGAROOS.
SUPPOSEDLY THEY USED TO THINK WE WERE BORN SO EARLY SO THE BABY'S GIANT HEAD COULD FIT THROUGH THE BIRTH CANAL, BUT NOW THEY THINK IT HAS MORE TO DO WITH THE MOTHER NOT BEING ABLE TO TAKE IN ENOUGH CALORIES.
OR IT MIGHT BE THAT HUMAN SOCIAL INTER-ACTION IS SO COMPLEX THAT BABIES NEED TO BE EXPOSED TO IT SO MUCH EARLIER THAN, LIKE, A PUPPY DOES. WILD, HUH?
I FORGET, DO YOU GUYS DISCOURAGE THE BABY-TALK THING? I ADMIT I'M NOT A BABY GUY BUT IT'S SO HAWD NOT TO DO, IDN'T IT? ♫ IDN'T IT, WIDDOW BEBE??
NO, IT'S FINE. BUT... RITU'S A LITTLE BUSHED SO MAYBE IT'S...
HEY HEY HEY!
WHERE IS SHE? LEMME AT'ER!

ALLOW ME TO INTRODUCE CHLOE SALILA GABER, EARTH'S NEWEST INHABITANT.
OH-EM-EFFING-GEE! LOOK AT YOU!!
CONGRATULATIONS, MAN. GOOD WORK.
THANKS, MAN.

OOOH, COME HERE, YOU! OOOH...
HELLO! HELLO! YES, YOU! YOU!
HOW MUCH DOES SHE WEIGH?
I THINK RITU SAID TWENTY-TWO POUNDS, I THINK?
WHAT?? TWENTY-TWO INCHES! SHE'S JUST UNDER SEVEN POUNDS.
I DON'T KNOW, I JUST MET HER!

MAMA'S LITTLE SEVEN POUND FATTY, THAT'S WHAT YOU ARE!
AREN'T YOU??
HEY, YOU GUYS WANT TO RUN TO THE DELI WITH ME REAL QUICK?

WHOA WHOA WHOA:
WHAT ABOUT ALL THAT BABIES-WILL-CHANGE-YOUR-LIFE-FOREVER PROPAGANDA YOU PARENTAL TYPES HAVE BEEN PUSHING?
YEAH! MATHEMATICALLY, YOUR HEART SHOULD BE SIX TIMES BIGGER THAN OURS!
LITERALLY.
THEY DO-- AND IT IS, BUT THIS FIRST STAGE IS THE WORST PART.
INFANTS SUCK.
BUT-- THIS IS THE TIME THEY MOSTLY LAY AROUND COOING AND LOOKING ADORBS, RIGHT?

DON'T GET ME WRONG: I ALREADY LOVE HER SO MUCH I WOULD MURDER EACH OF YOU, BUT WHEN THEY'RE THIS SMALL THEY'RE CRYING, POOPING MESSES.
YEAH, I REMEMBER WHEN I TRIED TO GET A SECOND CAT FOR BELVEDERE. OY!
YOUR LIFE GOES TOPSY TURVY, YOU'RE EXHAUSTED, YOU-- CHRIST, PLUS THIS TIME WE'LL HAVE BRAIDEN.
WHO KNOWS HOW HE'LL REACT TO ALL THIS?
BUT IT ALL WORKS OUT. I DON'T RECALL YOU GUYS HAVING TOO BAD A TIME WITH BABY BRAIDEN.
"NO FAMILY IS HOW IT APPEARS ON THE OUTSIDE."
CLUNK
EXIT
breath

IT SOUNDS CORNBALL, BUT PARENTHOOD REALLY IS ONE OF THOSE TRANSCENDENTAL EXPERIENCES. NOT IN A BLISSFUL WAY, PER SE, JUST IN THE SENSE THAT, YOU KNOW, WORDS FAIL.
IT'S LIKE YOUR FIRST LOVE OR...
OKAY, YOU LOVE CHOPS, RIGHT? I'M ASSUMING?
YOU ASSUME CORRECT. -LY.

WHY?
"WHY?" WELL, HE'S, LIKE...
I DON'T KNOW, HE... HMM.
DON'T TELL HIM! HE'S TRICKING YOU!

ANYONE WHO TELLS YOU PARENTHOOD IS ALL HUGS AND "LITTLE HOUSE ON THE PRARIE" AND SOCCER GAMES IS A FILTHY FUCKING LIAR. YOU'RE GOING TO BE STRESSED, YOU'RE GOING TO WORRY, YOU AND MARCY ARE GOING TO GET INTO FIGHTS ABOUT WHO LEFT THE STUFFED FROG AT THE PLAYGROUND.
YOU JUST HANG ON, CUZ YOU'RE SOMEONE'S DAD NOW, AND THAT'S WHAT DADS ARE SUPPOSED TO DO.

BUT... IT ALL WORKS OUT IN THE END, RIGHT?
I'LL LET YOU KNOW WHEN IT'S OVER.
HOW COME YOU CAN MAKE CHILD/PET ANALOGIES BUT WHEN I DO IT I'M THE ASSHOLE?

WELCOMETOBURGER TIMEWHEREITSALWAYS TIMEFORABURGER MAY IHELPTHE FOLLOWING CUSTOMER?

YEAH... I'LL HAVE A DOUBLE CHEESEBURGER, SWEET POTATO FRIES, A LARGE DIET COKE AND ... THAT'S IT.

UH, REGULAR FRIES, A PLAIN HAMBURGER, A DIET GRAPE SODA... AND A DOUBLE CHEESE BURGER AND A DIET SPRITE.
NOTHING ON THE BURGER. JUST MEAT AND BREAD.

LEMME HAVE A BACON CHEESE, UH, WAFFLE FRIES, A ROOT BEER...
HOLD THE ONIONS ON THAT, PLEASE.
THANKYOU YOUREORDER SEVENTYONE.

YOU KNOW I'LL ADMIT THAT I ACKNOWLEDGE THAT MY DECISION TO REFRAIN FROM BREEDING IS VERY UNNATURAL.
YOU DO?
WELL, SURE, THE WAY YOU DO IT.

IN THE EVOLUTIONARY SCALE OF THINGS..
OH! BEFORE I GO ON LET ME CLARIFY THAT WHEN I SAY "UNNATURAL" I DO NOT MEAN "BAD."
MOST OF HUMANKIND'S GREATEST ACCOMPLISHMENTS THWART NATURE'S INSIDIOUS PLANS: ANTI-BIOTICS, VACCINES, UH...
SPACE EXPLORATION, GUMMI BEARS, LITHIUM...

TXT T DENISE: Can't do it. Hol_
THE BATTERIES OR THE ANTI PSYCHOTIC?

BOTH!
NATURE IS A SURLY CUNT WHO IS TRYING TO KILL US AT EVERY TURN!

OKAY, SO THE PRINCIPLE OF LIFE ON EARTH IS EVOLUTION, RIGHT? THE CREATURES BEST SUITED TO THEIR ENVIRONMENT GET TO PASS ON THEIR GENES, RIGHT?
ORDER SIXTY-SEVEN!

SO, FOR ME, A PRIVILEGED, WHITE PERSON LIVING IN THE WEALTHIEST NATION ON THE PLANET..AMERICA.. FOR ME TO..
WAIT, SO YOU'RE SAYING ONLY RICH WHITE PEOPLE SHOULD HAVE BABIES?

YES, SCOTTY, ONLY RICH, WHITE AMERICANS SHOULD HAVE BABIES. IF WE'RE EVER GOING TO GET THIS MASTER RACE OFF THE GROUND WE HAVE TO GET SERIOUS.
WHAT I MEAN IS THAT ON A GLOBAL SCALE ALL AMERICANS ARE "FABULOUSLY WELL-TO-DO."
THE PEOPLE ON "THE WIRE" LIVE MATERIALLY BETTER LIVES THAN 75% OF THE PLANET.
PROBABLY NOT BUBBLES.
... SO FOR ME? A RELATIVELY WEALTHY AMERICAN WHOSE KIDS WOULD HAVE A VERY GOOD CHANCE OF SURVIVING AND PASSING ON MY GENES?
FOR ME TO PURPOSELY TAKE MYSELF OUT OF THE BABY GAME IS NOT ONLY UNNATURAL, IT'S DOWNRIGHT PERVERSE!
ORDER NUMBER SIXTY-NINE! WHO'S WAITING FOR SIXTY-NINE!
Hee Hee Hee!
THAT'S ME. I'M SIXTY-NINE.
Heh Heh!

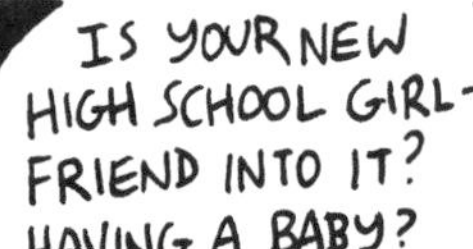
IS YOUR NEW HIGH SCHOOL GIRL-FRIEND INTO IT? HAVING A BABY?

OOH! YOU GUYS TOTALLY SHOULD DO IT!
THE THREE OF US NEW DADS WITH OUR BABY BJORKS LIKE IN ALL THOSE SHITTY MOVIES!

WELL, AS MUCH AS SHE HAD A BODY BUILT FOR MOTHERHOOD, IT DIDN'T QUITE PAN OUT FOR MICHELLE AND ME.
AW, IT'S OVER? DID SHE START SEEING THAT GUY FROM HER BIO CLASS?

NO, IT TURNS OUT SHE'S SEEING THIS DUDE SHE SLEEPS NEXT TO: HER HUSBAND.

SEVENTY!
RIGHT HERE!
HUSBAND? DIDN'T YOU SAY SHE WAS LIKE DIVORCED OR--?
I DID SAY THAT, BUT IT TURNS OUT WHEN SHE SAID IT SHE WAS LYING. HUSBAND-O-RAMA.

WOW.
BUT ISN'T THAT KIND OF, LIKE, PERFECT? YOU AREN'T LOOKING FOR A SERIOUS, LIKE, RELATIONSHIP.
THIS WAY YOU GET ALL OF THE PERKS BUT NONE OF THE OBLIGATION.
IT'S A CLASSIC FREE-MILK SCENARIO. ENJOY IT!

YEAH, BUT I DON'T KNOW. IT'S WEIRD. I FEEL WEIRD ABOUT IT.
THERE'S PLENTY OF DESPERATE MIDDLE-AGED WOMEN OUT THERE. I DON'T NEED TO BE BANGING AROUND WITH SOME OTHER DUDE'S WIFE.
IT'S JUST WEIRD.

OH, BOY, HERE IT COMES:
ALL RISE! JUDGE BROWNLOWE IS BACK IN SESSION!

WHAT, I'M A JERK BECAUSE I DON'T WANT TO WRECK SOMEONE'S MARRIAGE?
YOU GUYS HAVE WIVES, YOU SHOULD BE APPLAUDING MY MORAL STANCE!
BESIDES, AFTER..

YOU'RE ALWAYS--
???
YOU HOLD EVERYONE TO THESE RIDICULOUS, ARBITRARY STANDARDS AND IF THEY DON'T LIVE UP TO YOUR FUCKING, UH, LOFTY EXPECTATIONS THEN CLEARLY IT'S BECAUSE THEY--
YOU ACT LIKE THEY'RE THE ASSHOLES!
MEANWHILE, YOU'RE LIKE THIS, UH, DIVORCED STONER WHO LIVES OFF MONEY HIS GRANDMOTHER EARNED! WHO ARE YOU TO THROW FUCKING STONES??
GET THE FUCK OVER YOURSELF, WOULD YOU?
WHOA WHOA WHOA! TIME OUT! WHAT--
WHAT? I'M JUST SICK OF IT, YOU KNOW?
SICK OF HIM JUDGING EVERYONE AND EVERYTHING, LIKE HE'S SO GODDAMNED PERFECT, LIKE HE'S THE FUCKING, UH, UH, STANDARD-BEARER OR SOMETHING!
"STANDARD-BEARER??" WHAT DO YOU EVEN--??

FIRST OFF, A STANDARD-BEARER IS THE GUY WHO CARRIES A FUCKING FLAG NOT SOMEONE WITH--
OH! THANK YOU FOR EDUCATING ME AND PROVING MY POINT TH--
SECOND OF ALL--
(YOU'RE A TEACHER, RIGHT? YOU'D THINK YOU WOULD--ANY WAY:)
SECOND OF ALL: DON'T TAKE IT OUT ON ME IF YOU'RE PISSED OFF ABOUT HOW YOUR OWN LIFE HAS TURNED OUT AND HOW YOU'RE STUCK IN A MARRIAGE TO A WOMAN YOU CAN BARELY STAND AND ANOTHER SCREAMING BRAT TO--
HEY, G C'MON, EVER CALM DOWN
WHAT THE FUCK DID YOU--
I'M JUST SAYING THAT YOU USED TO BE MORE FUN TO HANG OUT WITH BEFORE YOU TURNED INTO THIS WHINING, PUSSY-WHIPPED CRYBABY WHO JUST COMPLAINS ALL--
"WAAH! ANOTHER BABY! YOU GUYS DON'T KNOW HOW HARD IT IS!"

YOU KNOW WHAT? FUCK THIS. FUCK THIS AND FUCK YOU.
SORRY, MAN, BUT THE WORLD NEEDS ADULTS, TOO. BUT HAVE FUN PLAYING PIRATES.
BILLY, I'LL SEE YOU BACK AT THE HOSPITAL. YOU KNOW, THAT BIG BUILDING WHERE MY NEW DAUGHTER'S WAITING.

WHAT... WHAT THE HELL WAS THAT ALL ABOUT??

IS THERE SOMETHING GOING ON WITH YOU TWO THAT I DON'T KNOW ABOUT?

ME?? HE'S THE ONE WHO STARTED IT! YOU HEARD HIM!

I KNOW, BUT... HE'S UNDER A LOT OF STRESS, AND YOU CALLED HIS KIDS BRATS. YOU CAN'T--

HIS KIDS ARE BRATS AND YOU KNOW IT! AND WHY ARE YOU TAKING HIS SIDE?

AND WHERE THE FUCK IS MY GODDAMN HAMBURGER??!

Manh
THAT'S WEIRD.

BUT SURELY THEY'VE GOTTEN INTO THESE KIND OF ARGUMENTS BEFORE, RIGHT?
I'M SURE IT WILL PASS AND YOU GUYS WILL BE BACK ON THE BOX BALL COURT LIKE NOTHING HAPPENED.
EX

MAYBE. HOPEFULLY.

BUT... I DON'T KNOW.
I MEAN, YOU'RE RIGHT, WE'VE ALL HAD OUR PISSY MOMENTS BUT THIS TIME THEY BOTH...
IT GOT REAL PERSONAL REAL QUICK, YOU KNOW?

I FEEL LIKE THIS SECOND KID HAS THROWN SCOTTY AND RITU BOTH OFF THEIR EQUILIBRIUM A BIT. THINGS WILL SETTLE DOWN.
BABY CHLOE IS SUPER-CUTE, RIGHT?
EVEN YOU HAVE TO ADMIT THAT!

YOU'RE PROBABLY RIGHT. THEY'RE PROBABLY JUST BLOWING OFF STEAM, RIGHT?
I JUST HOPE IT'S NOT AN OMINOUS SIGN OF THINGS TO COME.
Sigh
WHY DOES EVERYTHING HAVE TO CHANGE?

SORRY, BUT THAT'S KIND OF WHAT THE UNIVERSE DOES.
LOOK AT IT THIS WAY: IF THINGS DIDN'T CHANGE NONE OF US WOULD BE HERE AND WE'D STILL BE WEARING BANANA CLIPS.
212

I SUPPOSE SO.
BUT, HAHA, BUT ENOUGH ALREADY, RIGHT? FROM NOW ON WE ALL AGREE TO KEEP THINGS JUST THE WAY THEY ARE!

AWW, POOR BABY...

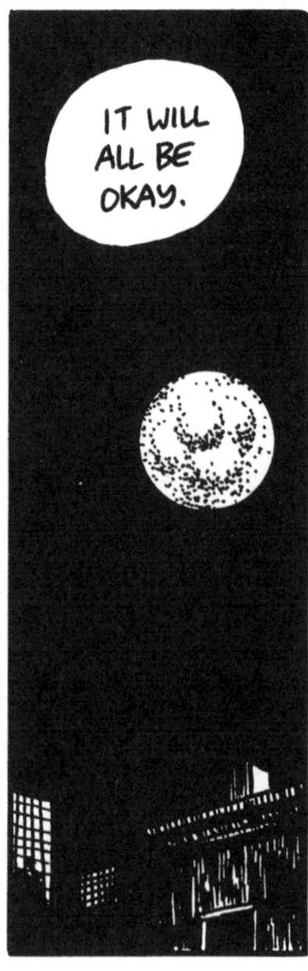
IT WILL ALL BE OKAY.

the SIRENS of BROOKLYN

Marcy: Okay, does anyone else need a refill before we start the movie? Julie?

Julie: I'm good.

Ritu: More wine!

(general laughter)

Nicole: I'm getting up anyway. I'll help you, Marce.

Ritu: Don't worry, I pumped before I left.

Kim: Oh my God, she is so cute. Admit it: you were happy to get a girl.

Ritu *(sheepish)*: I kind of was. I was starting to feel outnumbered by all those Y chromosomes. Plus I can finally buy girlie outfits.

Kim: We still have some of Louisa's old stuff if you want to take a look.

Ritu: Oh, really? I thought you and Nicole were thinking about having another one...?

Kim: Yeah, that isn't going to happen *(drinks)*.

Nicole: The trick with sangria is that you really have to start it the night before, you know?

Marcy: Yeah, you mentioned that in your e-mail yesterday. Hey, how's Louisa doing?

Nicole: I know a lot of people think you can just chop up a bunch of fruit and plop it in there but there's a real art to it.

Marcy: I saw those pictures from her birthday on Facebook. How old is she now? Nine?

Nicole: Yeah, she just—hold up: those aren't peaches are they? I thought I'd said in my e-mail that you should use—

Marcy: Oranges. They're oranges. Here you go. So, did you guys have, like, a party with all her friends from school? God, remember those parties? When you were a kid? Cupcakes and punch and everything? She has friends, right? I mean, I don't mean that she doesn't have friends, I just mean—but she's popular, right? Not in a snobby way but—

Nicole *(sipping)*: Mmm. Mmm. Yes, I gotta say, Marcy, this is really good sangria. Nicely done, my dear!

Marcy: Only because I followed your recipe to the letter!

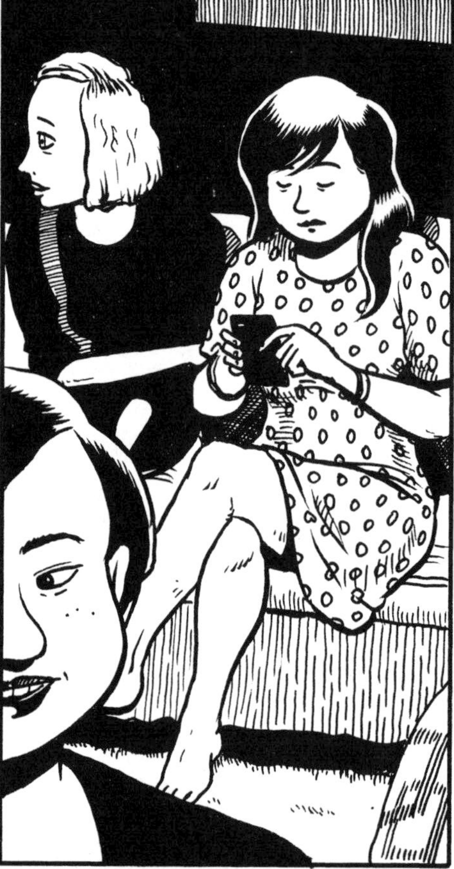

Dani: Yeah, her teacher said she was one of the best in the class. We're signing up for the intermediate lessons in the fall.

Kim: So cute. We're looking into—

Dani: I know, I know, they tell everyone that but she is really good and the teacher thinks she has real potential.

Kim: Wow, that's great.

Dani: Like, real potential.

Kim: That is such a cute top.

Dani: Ugh, I'm a pig.

Ritu: So we're next in line but it's taking forever so at one point Braiden toddles over to these Williamsburg hipsters and just goes like "Hiiii! " and gives this little wave.

Marcy: Awww.

Nicole: So cute.

Ritu: Right?? But this guy with his gross beard and Price is Right t-shirt just looks up from his phone and like literally scoffs. *(makes scoffing sound)* and goes back to playing his Angry Birds or whatever.

Nicole: What?!

Ritu: I know, right? So I made a point of telling Braiden—loud enough for the hipsters to hear—that sometimes people are rude and can't take a minute out of their day to be nice and so on.

Marcy: Haha, you actually said that? Loud enough for them to hear you?

Ritu: Yes. It was a little obnoxious, I admit, but what kind of jerks scoff at an adorable little boy?

Marcy: The adorablest little boy.

Nicole: Oh, and by the way you look great. You'd never guess you just had a kid.

Ritu: Blergh, I'm a hog.

Dani: Holy shit, that's amazing!

Julie: Yes, I figure this is my last time hanging out with you bridge-and-tunnel scum! *(clinks glass with Dani)*

Gina: What's going on?

Dani: Oh my god, they accepted Julie and Ken's bid on that place in Chelsea.

Julie: Yep, I signed on the line that is dotted on Tuesday.

Dani: That's amazing. That place was so cute.

Gina: Hey, do you know if they've found anyone for your old place? My stupid roommate is moving in with her boyfriend and I either have to find a new roommate or a new place.

Julie: Sweathog has a boyfriend? Wow. I thought you guys were planning on a whole Grey Gardens thing. Good for her!

Dani: Just goes to show you, there's someone for everyone.

Ritu: No way. We're done. I would've told the doctor to tie up my tubes while he was down there but Scott never left us alone together.

Nicole: Haha, he was suspicious.

Kim: How is Braiden handling it? Any drama?

Ritu: Ha! There's always drama. I think he's using our guilt. Well, Scott's guilt. I've been doing what all the books say to do but Scott's been buttering him up with toys and stuff.

Nicole: The best part of those books was that they confirmed what I always believed: my folks had no idea what they were doing.

Ritu: Yes, it's great that our generation is finally doing it correctly, right?

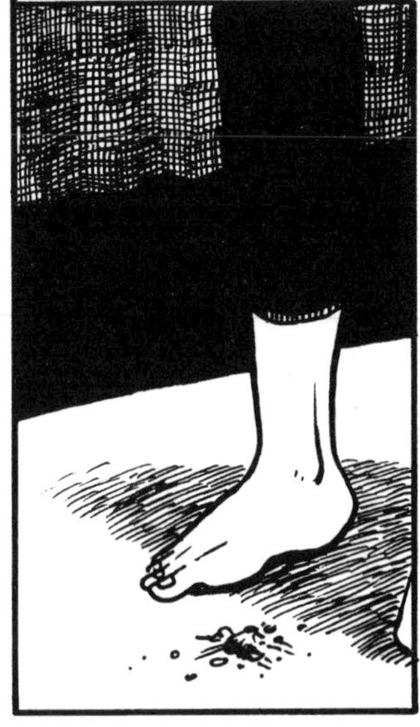

Gina: Look at how tan you are!

Kim: Yeah, we just got back from Montauk yesterday . It's weird: after years of everything being small businesses they built a 7-Eleven. I was really bummed, but it was nice to be able to get coffee in the morning.

Dani: For, like, three years we've been promising to Wyoming we'd take her to Disney, so it looks like this is the year. But it's good, right? Because she's really into the whole princess thing.

Gina: Oh my god! I went there with my nieces and they loved it. Skip Epcot, though, it's a drag.

Julie: Hey, don't discount Epcot. It's the only spot you can get beer in the whole place.

Ritu: So, Marce, are you going to, you know, make any big announcements?

Marcy: Hm? *(staring in Ritu's eyes while forcing a smile)* Oh, I already told them: I put out these great gluten-free pigs-in-a-blanket I found at the Fairway.

Kim: Oh, really? Where are they?

Marcy: Oh, right over here. *(catches Ritu's eyes again as she walks away)*

Ritu *(realizing she almost spilled the beans)*: Oh, yeah, they're great.

Gina: Well, yeah, I've been kind of...um, seeing someone. Romantically.

(general noise of happy excitement)

Ritu: I knew it!

Nicole: Oh, that's great, Gina.

Kim: How did you guys meet?

Dani: What does he look like? Let's see pics!

Gina *(sheepish)*: Well, I don't want you guys to make a big deal out of—

Julie: Oh my god! It's someone famous isn't it?

Gina:—it but it's, um, it's Eric.

(general noise of unease)

Ritu: What.

Kim: Um, the same Eric who...?

Gina: I know, but—

Ritu *(furious)*: How can you—

Marcy *(waving Ritu down)*: Okay, before we get all judgey: Gina, what's the story? How did you wind up back with, uh, with this guy?

Gina: He texted me, okay? He wanted to meet up and get some coffee or whatever and just...hang out. We met at Gorilla and talked about everything that happened between us and—

Ritu: "Everything that happened between you?" like what, the time he almost broke your nose?

Gina: That was just one time! He—

Ritu: "Just—??" How many times do you—?

Marcy *(waving Ritu down again)*: Okay, okay. So...what happened? Are you guys, what, officially back together or what's—

Gina: He's changed, okay? I know it sounds like a Lifetime movie cliché but it's true. He went to counseling and got anger management therapy and everything. He knows he majorly screwed up last time but he wants to try again. And he really has changed.

Kim: And...you want to try again, too?

Gina: Yes.

(looks all around as no one—or almost no one—is sure how to proceed)

Marcy:

Gina: Believe me, you guys, I totally understand where you guys are coming from but I think this is...I feel like I should give him a second chance, you know? It just feels different this time, it feels right. We're both different people now. And I...I can handle it.

Nicole: But be careful, Gin. If he gets out of line even once I want you to call us.

Kim: For real.

Julie: Fuck that, call the police.

Gina: I know and he won't. You guys, seriously, we totally talked about it and he really is different. You'll see.

Ritu: You guys are joking, right? Gina, honey, you aren't—you can't really be thinking about doing this, can you? Having that, that, asshole back in your life? He fricking punched you in the face!

Gina *(resolved)*: That was before.

Ritu *(sputtering)*: You keep saying that but that doesn't matter! Violence is a one-strike-you're-out deal!

Dani: I hate to say it, Gin, but...I think Ritu might be right. You deserve so much better, you know what I mean? You're beautiful, smart—not just beautiful on the outside but, like, inside. You deserve to be with a guy who treats you the way you deserve to be treated, you know?

Gina: But—

Kim: I totally agree.

(everyone starting to express agreement about how Gina is special, deserves better, etc.)

Kim: What about that guy you were just seeing? The Wall Street guy?

Julie *(grimaces comically)*: Ooh, with the hair? Eeesh.

Dani: Oh, okay, maybe not Wall Street guy!

(general amusement at the memory of Gina's date with the Wall Street guy)

Marcy: Oh! There' s a new guy at the hospital who seems nice.

Dani *(speaking the way one tries to get a small child excited)*: Ooh, a doctor?

Marcy: Umm, no, he's an administrator and, uh, actually, when I think about it he might be a little too old. But I'm sure we can—

Gina *(very loud)*: Would you guys shut up about it already? You don't know what the hell you're talking about!

(all in shocked silence)

Gina: I'm thirty-six years old, okay? You guys are all acting like there's this unlimited, uh, uh, pool of great single guys out there but guess what? There isn't, okay? You guys don't know because none of you have been single for, like, a thousand years but I know. You're all safe and snuggled and, uh, uh, in your perfect relationships but don't you think I want all that, too? I want to have a baby and take them to music classes and see them in school plays and I want a husband to run out to get me cough medicine at 2 a.m. when I'm sick and all of that stuff you guys have but it's last call, okay? I'm not twenty-five years old anymore and I'm sick of going on an endless stream of shitty dates with the losers my friends try to be nice and set me up with. I can't sit around waiting for some, uh, perfect guy to show up anymore.

Ritu: Honey, no one says he has to be per—

Gina: I know you guys think it's a big joke and I'm this pathetic, single ditz and you guys love hearing the stories of my pathetic dates, okay, and, oh, ha ha, what sad weirdo is she going out with his week but I'm not doing it anymore, okay? So, uh, you know, save your concern and your pity and your little jokes because, like, I'm done.

(all blindsided by outburst)

Gina: Thank you for the food, Marcy.

Julie: Gina, wait.

(Later. All of the women have left except for Marcy and Ritu, who are cleaning up.)

Marcy: That was—that was crazy, right?

Ritu: You know Gina. Her whole life is always a storm of drama.

Marcy: The worst part is that...I think she's probably right.

Ritu: What, about Eric? Because he—

Marcy: Not about Eric, but about us kind of looking down on her.

Ritu: Do you look down on her? I don't think I do. Do you?

Marcy: Well, no, but you have to admit we all have a kind of gleeful, I don't know, *schadenfreude* about her love life. We all love gossiping about her terrible dates and stuff.

Ritu: Ugh, remember that guy who was all into those Japanese comic books?

Marcy: Haha! Exactly! We're terrible people!

Ritu: Maybe. Or maybe we're all in long-term relationships with all that implies, and hearing Gina's sob stories reminds us that, whatever compromises we make and whatever complaints we might have about our spouses, being single isn't necessarily as fun as we might fantasize.

Marcy: Maybe.

Ritu: Here, let me get that. You should be resting, mama.

(Ritu moves chairs back around the table, completing the clean up.)

Ritu: Talking of which, I'm sorry if I embarrassed you before with the whole "big announcement" thing. I just thought you'd be excited to share the big news.

Marcy: Oh, it wasn't a big deal. I just didn't want to, you know, steal your thunder about baby Chloe.

Ritu: "Steal my—?" You're crazy. You should tell whoever you—wait, have you told anyone? Other than Scott and I?

Marcy *(sheepish)*: No.

Ritu: Wow, you got some willpower . Not even your parents or Billy's?

Marcy: Not a soul. I don't know why, really. It just...I mean, I do know why but it...it's just weird.

Ritu: "Weird?" What do you mean? Weird like—?

Marcy: I don't know, you know? I guess part of me is just kind of, like, scared.

Ritu *(relieved)*: Oh, honey, ev—

Marcy: Not scared like something will go wrong *(nervously taps wooden arm of the couch)*...I mean, I'm nervous about that, too, of course, but it's more like...I'm scared that...

Ritu: Just say it.

Marcy *(speaking slowly as she looks up at ceiling)*: Part of me is really worried...it feels like...

BILLY DOESN'T WANT THIS BABY.

Ritu: But, you—he said that? He actually said that?

Marcy: Not—not with his words but I know it's true. He acts like—what do I do? We—

Ritu: Oh, Marce, that's how guys are, you know? They want to hang on to that, like, Peter Pan bullshit forever. Trust me, Scotty was the exact same way with Braiden.

Marcy *(a grasp of hope)*: He was?

Ritu: Of course! I didn't tell anyone because, I don't know, I guess it was embarrassing, like it was somehow my fault. Or maybe I was afraid talking about it would mean it was true, or make it true.

Marcy *(sniffling)*: Yeah, I think I know what you mean. Am I just being an idiot?

Ritu: Yes, but a forgivable breed of idiot known as the first-time mother.

Marcy *(laugh of relief)*: Ha, *stultus expectatio mater*.

Ritu: But when Scotty first met him it was love at first sight. Billy will be the exact same way.

Marcy: Thanks, Ritu.

Ritu: Don't give it a second thought. Everything you're going through I've been through twice now, so you can always come to me. Scotty and I worked it out, you guys will too.

Marcy: I hope you're right.

Ritu: I'm always right. Ask Scotty.

"ROBERT?" MEH. "RICK?" I GUESS WE CAN ALWAYS FALL BACK ON NAMING HIM AFTER BILLY. "WILLIAM" HAS A LOT OF PERMUTATIONS. WILL. BILL. IS "LIAM" ONE? IT'S TECHNICALLY IN THERE.

HOW LONG UNTIL PEOPLE START OFFERING ME THEIR SEATS? THAT'S STILL A THING, RIGHT?

MARISSA. MELISSA. NO, THAT WILL REMIND ME OF MELISSA SAMPOGNIA FROM HIGH SCHOOL. MARGO. MARISOL. MARISOL? TOO DAINTY, IT SOUNDS LIKE PARISOL.

RUMINATION REVELATION

WEIRD THAT GIRL NAMES ARE SO SUBJECT TO FADS BUT BOY NAMES ARE RELATIVELY STATIC. SEXISM? BOYS=SERIOUS, GIRLS= FASHIONABLE, FLIGHTY?

WILL WE EVER HAVE A CHIEF JUSTICE NAMED TIFFANY? THEN AGAIN, WHO WOULD'VE IMAGINED WE'D HAVE A PRESIDENT NAMED BARACK HUSSEIN OBAMA?
crea

STILL, I HAVE TO ADMIT BEING DRAWN TO UNISEX OR EVEN BOYS' NAMES FOR A GIRL. DO I HAVE THE GUTS TO NAME MY DAUGHTER MICHAEL? OR JAMES? UGH, I CAN ALREADY HEAR MY MOM'S BARELY CONCEALED DISAPPOINTMENT.

SOME DAY I'M GOING TO BE MEETING THIS CHILD'S PROM DATE.
A LIMO WILL BE PULLING AWAY FROM OUR HOME FOR A NIGHT OF PARTYING -- PROBABLY DRINKING, MAYBE EVEN DRUGGING. BILLY AND I EXCHANGE A MEANINGFUL LOOK: OUR BABY ON THE THRESHOLD OF ADULTHOOD.

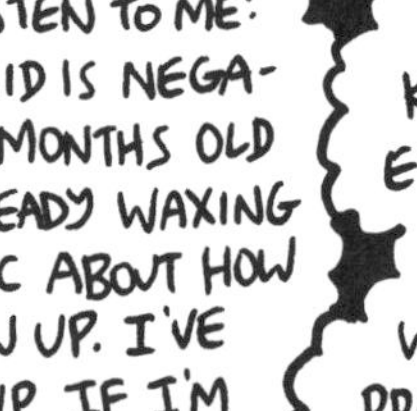
JEEZ, LISTEN TO ME: THE DARN KID IS NEGATIVE SEVEN MONTHS OLD AND I'M ALREADY WAXING MELANCHOLIC ABOUT HOW FAST IT GREW UP. I'VE GOTTA ZEN UP IF I'M GONNA DO THIS.

BESIDES: THE KID MIGHT NOT EVEN GO TO PROM.
MAYBE SHE WON'T GO AS A PROTEST AGAINST A SOCIAL INJUSTICE! GOOD FOR HER! SHE--
???

SCOTT! HEY, HOW'S IT GOING? WHAT BRINGS YOU TO THIS NECK OF THE WOODS?
WH--?? MARCY? Oh, HEY! WHOA, HEY, HOW'RE YOU? WOW, I-- WHAT A CRAZY-- WOW!

YEAH, JUST PICKING UP SOME BAKED GOODS 'N' COFFEE FOR THE CO-WORKERS. YOU SHOULD TRY THE DANISH, IT'S A HOME-RUN.
YEAH, YEAH, BILLY WAS SAYING THAT. COOL. SO...
I'M DENISE, BY THE WAY.
CHOKI

MARCY.
YEAH!
I'M SORRY,
DENISE THIS
MARCY. WE,
HEY.
LLY,
MEH!

YEAH, DENISE WORKS AT THE SCHOOL TOGETHER. I MEAN, WE, HaHa, WE BOTH WORK TOGETHER! AT THE SCHOOL. HaHa!
HEH. YEAH.

UH-HUH.
SO HOW'S BABY CHLOE SETTLING IN?

HMM?
OH! GREAT! YOU KNOW, WE'RE ALL, UH, ADJUSTING AND SO FAR BRAID'S HANDLING IT ALL LIKE A PRO! HAHA

DEBENEDETTO?

RIGHT HERE!
OKAY, GOTTA GO. SEE YOU AND RITU SATURDAY, RIGHT?
NICE TO MEET YOU, DENISE.
YEP.
BYE.

FUCK.
FUCKFUCK FUCKFUCKFUCK
HEY, IT'S OKAY. I DON'T THINK SHE--

ERGH! YOU FUCKING IDIOT! OUT OF ALL THE FUCKING PLACES TO GO YOU PICK...
AND YOU, WHAT, YOU HAD TO INTRODUCE YOURSELF?? YOU COULDN'T JUST
DON'T GET MAD AT ME!
IT WOULD'VE BEEN MUCH MORE SUSPICIOUS IF I DIDN'T SAY ANYTHING!
FUCK OKAY, OKAY, WHAT DO I DO? WHAT DO I DO?
LIKE YOU TOLD HER: WE'RE TWO CO-WORKERS OUT FOR COFFEE. IT'S NOT LIKE SHE BUSTED US CHECKING INTO THE PLAZA!
YOU'RE TOTALLY BEING, LIKE, ALL PARANOID.
HMM.
HMM. BILLY.
IF SHE SUSPECTS SHE'LL TELL BILLY FIRST.

I'LL TALK TO BILLY LATER. IF HE ACTS WEIRD I'LL KNOW SHE SAID SOMETHING TO HIM. THEN I CAN TELL HIM TO TELL MARCY NOT TO --
SCOTTY, SHE'S NOT GOING TO SAY ANYTHING. SHE--
YEAH, WELL, THAT'S EASY FOR YOU TO SAY, ISN'T IT? I'M THE ONE WITH SOMETHING TO LOSE IF SHE --
NEVER MIND. WE SHOULD GET BACK TO WORK.
YOU KNOW WHAT?
JUST TO BE SAFE LET ME GO AHEAD AND SIGNAL YOU WHEN IT'S ALL CLEAR, OKAY?
NO, YOU DON'T HAVE TO SIGNAL, BUT LEAVING SEPARATELY IS A GOOD IDEA. WE SHOULD ALSO --
DENISE?
WHAT THE HELL AM I GOING TO DO?

WHAT THE HECK DO I DO?

BUT YOU DIDN'T REALLY SEE ANYTHING, RIGHT? MAYBE THEY REALLY WERE JUST GETTING COFFEE LIKE HE SAID.

NO, NO, NO. THERE WAS DEFINITELY A, A VIBE.

A "VIBE?" WHAT DO YOU MEAN? LIKE..?

A VIBE! YOU KNOW! OKAY, REMEMBER THAT TIME WHEN WE FIRST STAYED AT MY PARENTS' PLACE AND THEY WENT OUT TO THE MOVIES BUT CAME BACK LIKE TEN MINUTES LATER BECAUSE MY MOM FORGOT HER SWEATER AND YOU SPRAINED YOUR ANKLE TRYING TO GET YOUR PANTS BACK ON BUT WE TRIED TO PLAY IT COOL? THAT KIND OF A VIBE.

OHHHH.

THAT SON OF A BITCH! HOW COULD HE CHEAT ON RITU AND NOT TELL ME??

WHAT? WHY?
IF THIS SITUATION WERE REVERSED AND SHE CAUGHT YOU ON A DATE WITH SOME SKANK I WOULD TOTALLY WANT HER TO TELL ME! YOU WOULDN'T?

BUT, MAR, YOU DIDN'T ACTUALLY SEE THEM DOING ANYTHING.
YOU CAN'T TELL SOMEONE THEIR SPOUSE IS CHEATING BASED ON A HUNCH.

IT WASN'T A HUNCH, IT WAS A VIBE.

I DON'T KNOW, COUNSELOR, YOU'RE ON SHAKY GROUND HERE.

ERRRRF

I SAY WE KEEP OUR HEADS DOWN AND MIND OUR BUSINESS ON THIS ONE.

"MIND OUR BUSINESS?" BUT IT'S TOTALLY OUR BUSINESS! THE SOCIAL CONTRACT MAKES IT OUR BUSINESS!
HAHA.. OKAY, HOW DOES THE SOCIAL..
OKAY, SO, SUPPOSE YOU FOUND OUT THAT I WAS HAVING AN AFFAIR WITH DR. KEPLER AT WORK, RIGHT?
NOW, IMAGINE THAT YOU ALSO FOUND OUT THAT SCOTTY KNEW ABOUT MY WEEKLY TRYSTS THE WHOLE TIME BUT DIDN'T TELL YOU.
HE SAYS IT "WASN'T HIS BUSINESS."
WOULDN'T YOU BE PISSED OFF AT HIM FOR NOT SAYING SOMETHING?

WAIT, WHICH ONE IS KEPLER? THE JACKASS WITH THE CIGAR BREATH?
HAIRY, CAVE-MAN TYPE?
COME ON! YOU KNEW MY WEAK-NESS FOR HUMMERS WHEN WE GOT MARRIED, BABY.
WELL?

WELL, OK, THAT WOULD BE...
BUT, HE ISN'T... OK, SEE, IN THIS CASE..

BZZZZZ

IT'S HIM! IT'S SCOTT!
What should I do??

Answer it!!

Exhale
HEY, MAN, WHAT'S UP?
...

YEAH, YEAH, ME, TOO. WH..
??

...
SURE, WE'RE LOOKING FORWARD TO IT. DO YOU NEED US TO..
...

MARCY? SURE, SHE GOT HOME ABOUT TWENTY MINUTES AGO.
DO, DO YOU WANT TO TALK TO HER OR..?
...

NO, NO, I JUST DIDN'T KNOW IF..
...
UH-HUH.
...

COOL, OKAY, SO WE'LL SEE YOU GUYS ON SATURDAY.
...
LATER.

BLEEP.

HE WAS SEEING IF WE'RE STILL ON FOR DINNER, AND...
HE ASKED HOW YOU WERE DOING.
AND??
THAT'S IT?
MARCY, HE NEVER ASKS HOW YOU'RE DOING.
Gasp!
HE WAS FISHING! TRYING TO FIGURE OUT IF I TOLD YOU ANYTHING!
FUCK.
WHAT, HE NEVER ASKS HOW I'M DOING?
SCREW HIM, I'M TOTALLY TELLING RITU.
DON'T SAY ANYTHING TO HER... PLEASE.
AT LEAST NOT YET.
FINE.
YOU MEN WITH YOUR DICKS.

DID YOU START READING IT YET?
HUH? OH, YEAH. I STARTED LAST NIGHT.

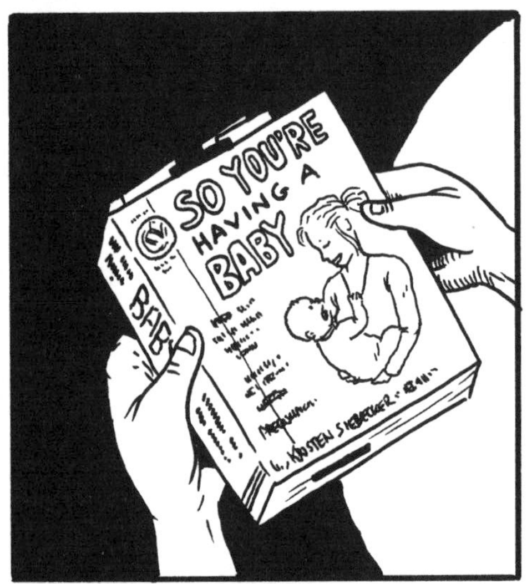
SO YOU'RE HAVING A BABY

FLIP
FLIP FLIP
FLIP FLIP
SO YOU'RE
BABY

BRICKBASHER 2
START
MENU

B

HULL BREACH
BAM!
SORRY, BRAH.
HAHA! OF COURSE HE'S CHEATING ON HER, THE JERK.
WHAT DOES HIS NEW CHIPPY LOOK LIKE? IS SHE CUTE?
HUH, I DON'T KNOW. I DIDN'T ASK AND MARCY DIDN'T TELL.
MARCY ALSO THINKS SHE SHOULD TELL RITU.
CLICK CLACK CLACKA CLICK
HAHA, RIGHT! SHE'LL SHIT A BRICK.
WAIT: YOU'RE NOT SERIOUS?
CLICKA CLACK CLICK

YOU GOTTA STAY OUT OF IT! BROS BEFORE HOS, AS THE KIDS SAY.
YOU DON'T BUY MARCY'S ARGUMENT? THAT SHE'D WANT RITU TO TELL HER?
LET'S CHECK OUT THAT BRIDGE.
LEVEL 9
NO, HER ARGUMENT IS VALID, SHE'S JUST MIXING IT UP:
WOULD YOU WANT RITU TELLING MARCY IF YOU WERE CHEATING?
ME?? OF COURSE NOT.
CLICK CLACK CLICK CLICK
THERE YOU GO, YOU HAD IT RIGHT THE FIRST TIME:
KEEP CALM AND SHUT THE FUCK UP.
UGH, WHAT A MESS.
OOH! PICK UP THAT MACE! IT WILL GIVE YOU ROBOT POWERS!
SO HAVE YOU EVER? CHEATED ON MARCY?

WHAT? NO.
CK
CLICK
CLICKA
CLACKA

NEVER? YOU GUYS HAVE BEEN TOGETHER A LONG TIME...
NO TIPSY KISSES AT THE OFFICE PARTY? NO ILLICIT HOOK-UPS WITH HER SISTER AT THE BEACH HOUSE...?

I REALLY WOULDN'T CALL A HANDJOB "CHEATING." IT'S REALLY LIKE A MEDICAL THINK A
WHAT THE WHAT??

KIDDING.
I'M GUESSING YOU DIDN'T CHEAT ON LISA OR YOU WOULD'VE SAID SOMETHING.
SHIT!

NO, I CHEATED ON LISA.

YOU DID??
WHAT'S WITH YOU GUYS? DO YOU HAVE A SUPER POWER THAT LETS YOU KEEP CRAZY SECRETS?!
IF I CHEATED ON MARCY I WOULD TOTALLY TELL YOU GUYS!

ANYWAY, I'M ASSUMING THIS IS RIGHT BEFORE YOU GUYS BROKE UP?
YOU WOULD THINK SO, BUT IT WAS RIGHT BEFORE WE GOT ENGAGED.
I GUESS THAT SHOULD'VE BEEN A WARNING SIGN, EH?

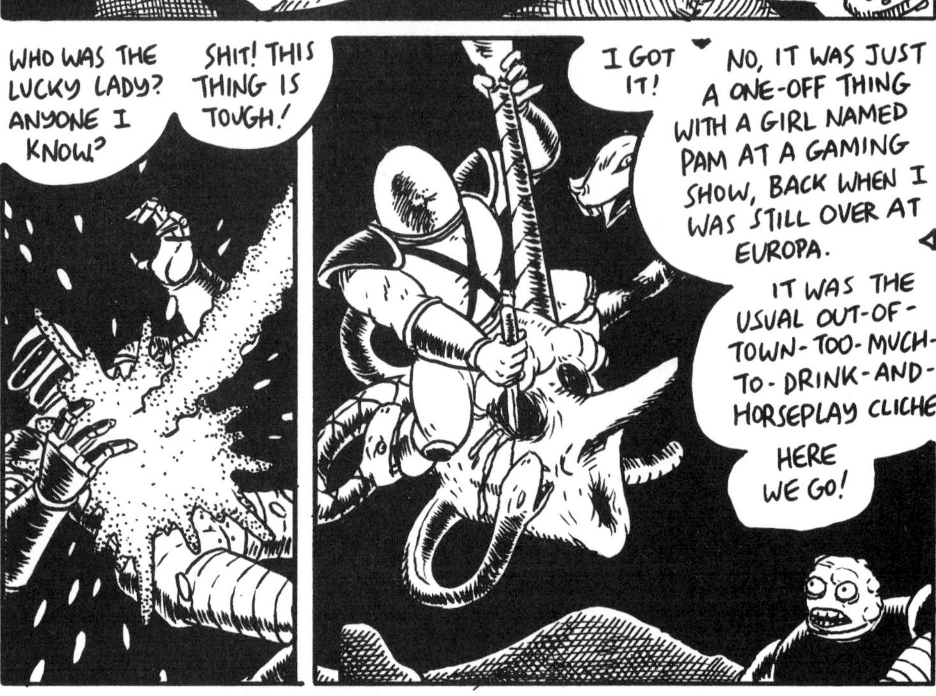
WHO WAS THE LUCKY LADY? ANYONE I KNOW?
SHIT! THIS THING IS TOUGH!
I GOT IT!
NO, IT WAS JUST A ONE-OFF THING WITH A GIRL NAMED PAM AT A GAMING SHOW, BACK WHEN I WAS STILL OVER AT EUROPA.
IT WAS THE USUAL OUT-OF-TOWN-TOO-MUCH-TO-DRINK-AND-HORSEPLAY CLICHE.
HERE WE GO!

DID LISA EVER FIND OUT ABOUT A GIRL NAMED PAM?
NO, AND I'M GLAD SOME BUSY-BODY DIDN'T SPILL THE BEANS AND WRECK EVERYTHING.

OR WRECK IT SOONER, AT LEAST.
LEVEL BREAK. WANT ANOTHER HIT?

WHAT'S UP FOR THE WEEKEND?
HERSCHEL AND I ARE GOING TO THE PLANETARIUM ON SATURDAY NIGHT.

PLANETARIUM? SERIOUSLY? IS IT LIKE A PINK FLOYD LASER SHOW OR SOMETHING?

NAH, METEOR SHIT.
YOU WANNA COME?

MARCE AND I HAVE, LIKE, A THING THAT NIGHT.
MAN, I HAVEN'T SEEN HERSCHEL IN, LIKE, FOREVER.

PHOOO
YEAH, ME, TOO. BUT WITH SCOTTY DEAD TO ME AND YOU HAVING THIS BABY I NEED TO BRING SOME MINOR LEAGUERS IN TO FILL MY BUDDY BENCH, Y'KNOW?
YOU WANT?

FOR SOMEONE WHO HATES SPORTS YOU LOVE BASEBALL METAPHORS.
AND YOU AND ME WILL STILL BE FRIENDS.

OKAY.
WHAT?? WE WILL!
I'M NOT ARGUING WITH YA.
READY TO TAKE A CRACK AT THE NEXT LEVEL?
I ONLY HAVE SOUR CREAM AND..
W.T. FUCK IS THIS NOW?
AHH, YOUR COUCH WAS REALLY KILLING MY BACK SO I'M JUST LAYING ON THE FLOOR FOR A SPELL.
JUST FOR A FEW MINUTES.
HAHA, YOU'RE A PIECE OF WORK.
ISN'T IT WEIRD THAT EVERY HUMAN ON EARTH IS A RESULT OF A MAN AND A WOMAN MAKING SWEET LOVE?
THERE'S, WHAT? TWO BILLION PEOPLE IN THE WORLD?
THAT'S, LIKE, A LOT OF FUCKING.

PLAYER ONE
CHOOSE WEAPON
NOT TO MENTION ALL OF THE SWEET LOVE-MAKING THAT (THANKFULLY) DOES NOT RESULT IN BABIES.
OKAY, I'M SWITCHING GUYS. I WANNA TEST DRIVE THE HOT BARBARIAN.
ARE YOU STICKING WITH LUMPY OR ARE YOU MIXING IT UP?
HAND ME MY CONTROLLER.
MY COMPTROLLER.
HAND ME MY STATE COMPTROLLER ALAN HEVESI.
Y'KNOW, I'M TAKING THE FACT THAT YOU DON'T WANT TO EXPOSE SCOTTY AS A FILTHY PHILANDERER AS PROOF THAT DEEP DOWN YOU STILL LOVE HIM.
SHIT, YOU'RE PROBABLY RIGHT. WHAT'S RITU'S NUMBER? I WANT TO--
WAIT, YOU'RE NOT USING THE RABBIT!

C'MON, YOU LOVE FURRIES, AND THIS GUY LOOKS TOTALLY BAD ASS!
I KNOW YOU AND SCOTTY ARE UNDER A LOT OF STRESS AT THE MOMENT, BUT ONCE THINGS SETTLE DOWN, COOLER HEADS WILL PREVAIL.
YOU'LL PATCH THINGS UP GOOD, I'LL WAGER.
(OKAY, I'M GOING WITH THE POWER GAUNTLET AND THE CRAB BLASTER.)
(OH, AND CAN I USE A PILLOW?)
HERE YOU GO, GRAMPS. SET?
FIRE WHEN READY, GRISWALD.
THE PROBLEM WITH YOUR THEORY IS THAT I'M NOT STRESSED OUT.
I'VE GOT THE THREE ESSES: SINGLE, STEADY EMPLOYMENT AND STONED.
COOL AS A CUKE, PAL.
(WAIT, IS THERE SOMETHING BEHIND THIS DOOR I NEED TO KNOW ABOUT?)

MORE IMPORTANTLY, JUST WHEN DO YOU THINK THINGS ARE GOING TO "SETTLE DOWN"? WHEN BABY ZOEY GOES TO KINDERGARTEN?
A FEW MONTHS FROM NOW WHEN YOU AND MARCY HAVE YOUR OWN BABY?
HOW ABOUT WHEN SCOTTY AND RITU OUTGROW THEIR PLACE AND MOVE TO THE SUBURBS?
(DON'T LET THAT GOO DRIP ON YOU)
THERE'S NO SETTLING DOWN, BUCKO. THIS IS IT.
RUBBISH.
A PERIOD OF ADJUSTMENT, YOU'LL SEE.
NOT TO GET TOO OPRAH ABOUT IT, BUT, IF ANYTHING, THIS SHOULD STRENGTHEN OUR BONDS-- MAKE US APPRECIATE THE FRIENDSHIPS WE MIGHT TAKE FOR GRANTED.
HO BOY.
NO, NO, FOR REALS. OUR UPTIGHT SOCIETY DOESN'T LET STRAIGHT GUYS EXPRESS FEELINGS BUT YOU KNOW WHAT?
FUCK THOSE GUYS!

YOU AND SCOTTY ARE BOTH IMPORTANT TO ME AND, WELL, I LOVE YOU.
I DIDN'T WANT TO SAY IT BUT YOU DRAGGED IT OUT OF ME: I LOVE YOU AND I LOVE SCOTTY.
900
THAT PUNCH WAS AMAZING, BUT YOU'RE MAKING ME, LIKE, PROFOUNDLY UNEASY, DUDE.
LET'S TONE DOWN THE BRAD GOODMAN-SPEAK AND FOCUS ON KILLING MONSTERS, HUH?
HAHA, MAYBE THE MONSTER YOU FEAR THE MOST LIVES IN YOUR OWN HEART.
MAYBE, BUT MAYBE WE--
IS YOUR CONTROLLER BUSTED? WHY ARE YOU NOT RUNNING?
I'M RESOLVING THE NEGATIVITY RIGHT HERE, RIGHT NOW.
CAN'T IT WAIT? THE NEXT ROOM IS THE SWAMP SEX ROBOT!

DUDE! WANDERING MONSTER!
HEY, SCOTTY, HOW'S IT GOING?
HEY, MAN, I WAS JUST GOING TO CALL YOU. WHAT'S UP?
KISS YOUR LONG-EARED VARMINT GOODBYE.
AHH, NOT MUCH. JUST OVER AT BROWNIE'S TAKING THE NEW "MURDEREALM" OUT FOR A TEST DRIVE.
IS THAT A VIDEOGAME OR STRAIN OF WEED?
UGH! FINE, I'LL KILL IT BUT I GET ALL THE POINTS!
HAHA, A LITTLE FROM COLUMN A, A LITTLE FROM COLUMN B...
CLICKA-CLK CLICK CLACKA CLICKACK

I WANTED TO TALK ABOUT--
YEAH, SO LISTEN: I WAS JUST TELLING OL' BROWNIE HERE THAT, UH, EVEN THOUGH I KNOW YOU GUYS ARE GOING THROUGH, LIKE, A, UH...
YOU KNOW...
ROUGH PATCH, THAT DEEP DOWN WAY DEEP INSIDE I KNOW YOU GUYS ARE STILL, UH, FRIENDS.
HAHA, WE ARE, ARE WE? WHY DO YOU SAY THAT?
CAN THIS INTERVENTION NOT WAIT FOR, LIKE, TWO MINUTES?? THIS GIANT-SIZED
CLICK CLICK CLACKA CLK
TWO THINGS:
A) WELL, FOR ONE THING, YOU GUYS HAVE BEEN BUDS FOR, LIKE, UH, FOREVER AND IT WOULD BE A REAL SHAME TO, YOU KNOW, LIKE, THROW THAT AWAY OVER SOME, LIKE, UH, UH, DUMB COMMENTS THAT MAY OR MAY NOT HAVE BEEN SAID IN, UH, YOU KNOW, IN, IN...
WE'RE ALL STRESSED OUT!
UH...

I HOPE YOU'RE SATISFIED. JERK.
MY ONLY CONSOLATION IS THAT NOW I GET TO WATCH THIS ASSHOLE ENERGY DRAIN YOUR
BUNNY
Y'KNOW, LIKE, REMEMBER THAT TIME WE ALL WENT TO MONTAUK AND THE FIVE OF US, UH, SHARED ONE ROOM AND WE WENT TO THAT BAR WHERE THE GUY CLAIMED HE, LIKE, INVENTED THE LONG ISLAND ICED TEA AND YOU HOOKED UP WITH THAT CHUBBY GIRL BUT YOU DIDN'T HAVE A CONDOM BUT BROWNIE HAD ONE IN HIS WALLET BUT IT WAS, LIKE, FIFTY YEARS OLD SO IT WAS ALL DRIED OUT AND, LIKE, DRIED OUT AND SHIT?
AND, LIKE, REMEMBER WHEN WE TRIED TO GET BACK TO THE ROOM BUT, UH, THE, UH, LIKE, SHE WAS A HOTEL DETECTIVE OR WHAT-EVER SO WE COULDN'T LET HER SEE THERE WERE FIVE OF US SO YOU AND BROWNIE, LIKE, SLEPT IN THE CAR?
GAME OVER
MENU
GOOD TIMES, RIGHT? YOU CAN'T JUST, UH, THROW ALL --
I'M FEEDING THE CAT.
MROW!
WHAT'S THE OTHER THING?
WHAT OTHER--?
Sigh
YOU SAID THERE WERE TWO THINGS THAT MADE YOU--

OH! RIGHT! THE SECOND THING IS THAT HE TOLD ME THAT HE AGREES WITH ME THAT MARCY SHOULDN'T SAY ANYTHING TO RITU AB--

UM

OKAY.
YEAH, SO I CAN'T REALLY TALK RIGHT NOW BUT LET'S MAKE A PLAN TO GET TOGETHER THIS WEEK, OKAY?

AND, LET'S KEEP IT ON THE D.L. UNTIL WE DISCUSS THE AGENDA, OKAY?
OKAY, BYE.

Sigh
I DON'T FEEL LIKE COOKING, DO YOU? WANNA GET TACOS?
WHAT WAS THAT ABOUT? EVERYTHING ALL RIGHT?

HMM? OH, YEAH, NOTHING. JUST, UH, SOME WORK STUFF. YOU KNOW.
I'M GONNA TRY PUTTING HER DOWN. TACOS ARE GOOD. ORDER ME A HUMUNGO.
'KAY.

BILLY?

SINCE WE ALWAYS SEE THE SAME SIDE OF THE MOON, IT'S EASY TO FORGET THAT IT ACTUALLY ROTATES.
IT USED TO MOVE MUCH FASTER AND SHOW EARTH ALL OF ITS SIDES, BUT EARTH'S GRAVITY HAS SLOWED IT DOWN TO THE POINT WHERE IT'S "TIDALLY LOCKED."
NOW, THE FAR SIDE OF THE MOON REMAINS FOREVER HIDDEN FROM VIEW.

OUR EXPANDING
Universe
HERSCHEL!
MY MAN!

ON THE DOWNLOW WITH MR. BROWNLOW!
SORRY I'M A LITTLE LATE. MOM MISSED THE EXIT SO I HAD TO TAKE THE NEXT TRAIN.
NO PROBLEM. WAIT A SEC: WHAT EXIT? AREN'T YOU STILL OUT IN GREENPOINT?
COSMI

HAHA, I SUPPOSE IT REALLY HAS BEEN A LONG TIME, HUH?
NO, LAST YEAR I HAD TO MOVE BACK TO ISLIP WITH MOM AFTER DOUBLECOURT LAID ME OFF.
AW, SHIT, THAT SUCKS. ARE YOU LOOKING FOR A NEW GIG OR--?

I LOVE THIS GUY.

ACTUALLY, IT'S A LADY.

SO I HEAR MARCY AND BILLY ARE TAKING THE PLUNGE.

THEY LIVE IN FILTH, THEY'RE SICK ALL THE TIME, THEY CAN BARELY FOCUS FOR THREE MINUTES IN A ROW...
ALL THEY TALK ABOUT ARE BABIES!
"MY OPINION ON THE SITUATION IN THE MIDDLE EAST? UM... DID I TELL YOU SAYLOR IS USING HIS BIG BOY POTTY NOW?"
YOU CAN HARDLY BLAME THEM ON THAT SCORE, DUDE. YOU REALLY CARE WHAT'S GOING ON IN THE MIDDLE EAST?
NO, BUT MORE THAN I DO ABOUT WHERE SAYLOR TAKES A SHIT!
BUT THE WORST PART IS THAT SMUG, CONDESCENDING TONE THEY USE WITH NORMAL PEOPLE, YOU KNOW?
"OH, YOU HAVEN'T TRIED HEROIN YET? AWWW.
"MAYBE ONE DAY YOU'LL BE BLESSED WITH A SYRINGE OF YOUR OWN."

THESE BREEDER TYPES ACT AS IF THEY'RE FULFILLING SOME NOBLE, HIGHER PURPOSE WHEN ALL THEY'RE DOING IS TAKING ORDERS FROM THEIR DNA.!
REPRODUCE! PASS ON YOUR GENES! MUST REPRODUCE!
AND THEN THEY COME UP WITH SOME HORSESHIT RATIONALE FOR THEIR ULTIMATELY SELFISH BEHAVIOR.!
WAIT, HOW EXACTLY IS IT SELFISH? YOU COULD SAY
OF COURSE IT IS! DEEP DOWN EVERYONE WANTS A TINY VERSION OF HER OR HIMSELF.
THEY SECRETLY WANT A TINY VERSION OF THEMSELVES SO THEY CAN UNDO ALL THE MISTAKES THEIR OWN PARENTS MADE RAISING THEM.

IT'S ODD: FOR SOMEONE WHO CLAIMS TO HATE KIDS YOU SEEM TO SPEND A LOT OF TIME COMING UP WITH ELAB-ORATE THEORIES ABOUT THEM.
:SIGH: WELL, I HAVE A LOT OF FREE TIME NOW THAT MY FRIENDS HAVE KIDS.
COSM
PLAN
RI
HAHA! THAT'S THE ENVIOUS, PUL-SATING HEART OF YOUR ARGUMENT, ISN'T IT?
WHEN IT COMES DOWN TO IT YOU JUST CAN'T STAND THAT SOMEONE ELSE IS DIVERTING ATTENTION FROM YOU.
HEY, WHOA! YOU MAKE ME SOUND LIKE SOME KIND OF SELF-CENTERED JERK!
NOW WILL YOU SHUT UP FOR TWO SECONDS AND LET ME TALK, FOR CHRIST'S SAKE?
I'M JUST CONCERNED BILLY'S DAUGHTER WILL BE GRADUATING COLLEGE BY THE TIME YOU FINISH.

PSSH! THAT KID AIN'T GOING TO NO COLLEGE!
WHERE DO YOU WANNA SIT?
OOH! LET'S GO NEAR THOSE PRETTY LADIES.
HehHeh,
"HELLO, GIRLS. HOW ABOUT I GIVE YOU AN OPPORTUNITY TO SATISFY YOUR CURIOSITY ABOUT MY MICRO ORGANISMS?"
WAIT, THAT DIDN'T COME OUT RIGHT.
EXCUSE ME, ARE THESE SEATS TAKEN?
ARE YOU SAVING THEM FOR YOUR BOYFRIENDS OR...?
EH, JEG BEKLAGER, MEN FOREGNER IKKE AT TALE ENGELSK?
FORSTÅR DU?
HAHA, WE SHOULD'VE GUESSED THE ONLY PEOPLE HERE ON A WEEKDAY AFTER-NOON ARE TOURISTS AND BUMS!
TRUE ENOUGH.
WHAT WAS I ABOUT TO..? OH, YEAH: KIDS.

TO SUM UP: THEY STINK, THEY'RE HERE TO REPLACE US, AND THEY'RE THE TRUE OPIATE OF THE MASSES:
A HANDY DISTRACTION TO KEEP PEOPLE FOCUSED ON THEIR OWN LITTLE NARCISSISTIC WORLD INSTEAD OF THE BIG, UH, PICTURE OR WHATEVER.
YOU ASK A PARENT HOW IT CAN POSSIBLY BE WORTH ALL THE STRESS AND BULLSHIT AND ALL THEY CAN BURBLE OUT ARE LAME PLATITUDES AND HALLMARK SENTIMENTS.
TO THE OUTSIDE OBSERVER IT RESEMBLES NOTHING SO MUCH AS GOOD OLD FASHIONED STOCKHOLM SYNDROME.
Whew
Heh Heh WOW.
CAN I REBUT NOW?
"REBUT?" WHOSE SIDE ARE YOU ON?
I WAS JUST VENTING! I'M NOT PREPARED TO DEFEND MY CRACKPOT IDEAS!
I, TOO, HAVE A THEORY, AND THAT THEORY IS THAT YOU COULD BE WRONG.
WRONG? I SHOULD SLAP YOUR FILTHY MOUTH.
GO ON.

NO, YOU'LL LIKE THIS. IT CONNECTS TO YOUR BIG "JUNKIE" HYPOTHESIS.
DO YOU RECALL WHEN WE WENT TO BURNING MAN AND YOU HAD THAT WHOLE PEYOTE FREAKOUT?
REMEMBER IT? IT WAS A WATERSHED MOMENT OF MY LIFE AND IT FOREVER ALTERED MY CONSCIOUSNESS AND CHANGED THE WAY I SEE THE WORLD.
OF COURSE I DON'T REMEMBER IT!
12 EARTH YEARS EARLIER
SO WHAT WAS IT LIKE? WHY DID IT CHANGE YOU SO MUCH?
DESCRIBE IT TO ME.
OKAY, WELL IT FELT, UH...
IT WAS LIKE I FELT, LIKE, CONNECTED TO, LIKE, UH, THE--
IT'S REALLY HARD TO PUT INTO WORDS. IT WAS JUST, LIKE, THIS PROFOUND... THING.
BUT IT WAS A REALLY PLEASURABLE EXPERIENCE?
HMM... I DON'T KNOW IF "PLEASURABLE" IS THE WORD I WOULD USE.
I MEAN, I'M GLAD I DID IT BUT THERE WERE DEFINITELY PARTS WHERE I WAS, LIKE, FREAKING OUT.

SO IT HAD ITS HIGHS AND LOWS BUT IT--

WAIT! ARE YOU ABOUT TO TELL ME YOU BROUGHT PEYOTE TO THE PLANETARIUM, YOU BEAUTIFUL GIANT MAN??

HAHA, EASY, KILLER.

ALL THAT I'M SAYING IS THAT TRANSCENDENTAL EXPERIENCES COME IN ALL SHAPES AND SIZES.

THINK OF PARENTHOOD AS A TWENTY YEAR DRUG TRIP. IT HAS HIGHS AND LOWS, MAKES YOU ACT BAT SHIT CRAZY AND FOREVER ALTERS HOW YOU EXPERIENCE THE WORLD.

I AM NOT GOING TO LET YOU RUIN HALLUCINOGENS FOR ME!

BESIDES, IT'S RIDICULOUS! YOU MAKE IT SOUND LIKE EVERY OPRAH HOUSEWIFE AND PEE-WEE FOOTBALL DAD IS ON SOME KIND OF, LIKE, VISIONQUEST!

WHAT CAN I TELL YOU? MOST PEOPLE ARE IDIOTS.

YOU CAN PUMP SOME MEATHEAD FRAT-BOY FULL OF L.S.D. BUT IT'S NOT NECESSARILY GOING TO CHANGE ANYTHING ABOUT HIS MINDS

Ladies and gentlemen, Welcome to the Tyson Planetarium...

UT! OFF WE GO!

WHEN YOU WERE BORN YOU DID NOT DISTINGUISH YOURSELF FROM THE WORLD AROUND YOU. YOU LITERALLY EXPERIENCED THE UNIVERSE-- YOUR BODY, YOUR PARENTS, THE ENTIRE WORLD--AS AN EXTENSION OF YOURSELF.
Saturn
JUPITER

THROUGHOUT MOST OF HUMAN HISTORY, WE SAW THE UNIVERSE AS UNCHANGING, STATIC AND ETERNAL.
THE MOON, THE PLANETS, THE SUN, THE STARS -- THEY ALL REVOLVED AROUND A FIXED CENTER: OURSELVES, THE EARTH.
The Sun
The Moon
MERCURY
MARS
Venus
IT'S HARD TO BLAME US. IT WAS COMFORTING, OF COURSE, BUT IT MADE PERFECT SENSE, AND FROM WHAT WE COULD SEE THERE WAS NO REASON TO THINK OTHERWISE.

IT WAS ONLY 500 YEARS AGO THAT A POLISH SCHOLAR NAMED MIKOLAJ KOPERNIK (BETTER KNOWN BY HIS ADOPTED LATIN NAME COPERNICUS) FIGURED OUT THAT EVERYTHING WE KNEW WAS WRONG...
Jupiter
Venus
Mars
Mercury
IT WAS ACTUALLY THE SUN AROUND WHICH EVERYTHING REVOLVED. THE EARTH WAS JUST ONE OF THE PLANETS ORBITTING A BRIGHT, FIERY SPHERE.
WE STRUGGLED WITH AND ADAPTED TO THE NOTION THAT WE WERE NO LONGER THE FIXED CENTER OF THE UNIVERSE.
Sol
Saturn
Earth
The Moon
IN FACT, WE WERE SLIGHTLY OFF CENTER -- AND HURTLING THROUGH SPACE AT TREMENDOUS SPEED.

THE INVENTION OF THE TELESCOPE IN 1608 CHANGED EVERYTHING. IN ITALY, SCIENTIST GALILEO GALILEI POINTED ONE INTO THE SKY, REVOLUTIONIZING ASTRONOMY AND (ONCE AGAIN) CALLING INTO QUESTION OUR PERCEIVED PLACE IN THE UNIVERSE.
AMONG HIS MANY DISCOVERIES, HE SAW THAT THE MILKY WAY-- PREVIOUSLY THOUGHT TO BE AN ENORMOUS CLOUD OF GAS-- WAS ACTUALLY AN ENORMOUS CLUSTER OF STARS.
WE WERE LIVING IN A GALAXY PACKED WITH SUNS, AND TODAY SCIENTISTS HAVE DISCOVERED OVER A THOUSAND PLANETS ORBITING THOSE ALIEN SUNS.
Class of 2029
PARADOXICALLY, THE UNIVERSE HAS BECOME EMPTIER AND MORE CROWDED THAN WE EVER IMAGINED.

IN THE 1920S AMERICAN ASTRONOMER EDWIN HUBBLE POINTED THE (THEN) WORLD'S LARGEST TELESCOPE AT THE ANDROMEDA NEBULA.
WHAT WAS THOUGHT TO BE A CLOUD OF DUST AND GAS INSIDE THE MILKY WAY TURNED OUT TO BE AN ENTIRELY DIFFERENT GALAXY ALTOGETHER -- ONE ALMOST AS BIG AS OUR OWN! AND THAT WAS JUST THE START!
AS IF THE DISCOVERY OF BILLIONS OF NEW STARS WASN'T ENOUGH, HUBBLE'S WORK REVEALED THAT ALL OF THESE NEWLY OBSERVED GALAXIES WERE ON THE MOVE -- AWAY FROM EACH OTHER.
THE UNIVERSE WAS EXPANDING!
THIS AMAZING DISCOVERY PROVIDED THE BASIS FOR A NEW THEORY SARCASTICALLY REFERRED TO AS THE "BIG BANG."
IN THEORY, YOU COULD TAKE THE MOTION OF GALAXIES AND EXTRA-POLATE BACKWARDS IN TIME.
THE FARTHER BACK YOU WENT, THE CLOSER AND TIGHTER THINGS WOULD GET.
REWIND ABOUT FOURTEEN BILLION YEARS AND THE ENTIRE UNIVERSE CAN FIT IN THE PERIOD AT THE END OF THIS SENTENCE.

NOW THE QUESTION WAS: HOW LONG WOULD THE EXPANSION LAST?

MANY ASSUMED THAT, AS TIME PASSED, GRAVITY WOULD EXERT CONTROL AND SLOW THE EXPANSION.

SOME EVEN SPECULATED THAT THE PROCESS WOULD EVENTUALLY REVERSE ITSELF, AND THAT THE UNIVERSE WOULD END IN A "BIG CRUNCH."

WE GOT AN ANSWER IN 1998.

BY OBSERVING DISTANT SUPER-NOVAE, A TEAM OF INTERNATIONAL ASTRONOMERS FIGURED OUT THAT THE EXPANSION WASN'T SLOWING DOWN AT ALL-- IT WAS ACTUALLY SPEEDING UP!

THE FARTHER AWAY A GALAXY IS, THE FASTER THE SPACE BETWEEN US GROWS...

AS TIME PASSES, THE LIGHT FROM OTHER GALAXIES WILL DIM AS THEY MOVE FARTHER AND FARTHER AWAY.
EVENTUALLY, THEY WILL JUST DISAPPEAR, HAVING MOVED SO FAR AWAY THAT THEIR LIGHT WILL NEVER REACH US.
THE MILKY WAY WILL BE A LONE ISLAND IN A SEA OF INFINITE DARKNESS.

Sigh
WELL, THAT CERTAINLY PUTS THINGS IN PERSPECTIVE.
OH, SHIT, IT LOOKS LIKE IT'S RAINING.

YEAH, TOO MUCH FUCKING PERSPECTIVE.
OH, I DON'T KNOW.
SOMETIMES BEING REMINDED YOU ARE COSMICALLY INSIGNIF-ICANT CAN BE VERY LIBERATING.
OKAY, MAN, TAKE CARE.
YEAH, LET'S TRY TO HANG AGAIN SOON.
IF I HEAR OF ANY GIGS I'LL LET YOU KNOW.

YOU DIDN'T TELL ME WE'D HAVE COMPANY.

OH, HAHA!

WE'RE A LITTLE SHORT-STAFFED AT WORK AT THE MOMENT, SO I'M BACK IN THE TRENCHES.

Heart to Heartless

HIS IS DENISE. SHE'LL
ILLING IN UNTIL MRS.
ORETTA GETS BACK
R "VACATION".
ELLO.!
RIDAY IF I CAN'T
RESS THE "NEXT"
TAKES YOU BAC
REEN, RIGHT? SO
VAS IT DOING
ST PLACE?
SO FUNNY! TH
TIME I GOT S
ROJECT DEADLIN
QUARTER.
SCOTTY,
HOW'S IT GOIN

WOW.
WOWOWOW.
SO... SHE KNOWS YOU'RE, LIKE, MARRIED AND ABOUT THE KID AND EVERYTHING?
KIDS PLURAL. BUT, YEAH,
BUT I NEVER PROMISED HER ANYTHING.
I NEVER SAID I WOULD LEAVE RITU OR ANYTHING. I WAS ALWAYS HONEST WITH DENISE ABOUT, YOU KNOW...
WHAT THIS IS. OR WAS.
OR WHATEVER.
NATURALLY. HONESTY IS THE CORNERSTONE OF ANY SUCCESSFUL RELATIONSHIP.
SO, WHAT'S THE, UH, STATUS OF... LIKE, ARE YOU STILL SEEING HER OR--?
NO, WE GOT INTO A BIG THING AFTER MARCY :Sigh: AFTER THAT THING WITH MARCY.
IT'S DONE.
OH, WELL THAT'S GOOD ... RIGHT?
I HAVE TO ADMIT THAT I'M STILL KINDA FREAKED OUT ABOUT THIS.
YOU WERE SEEING THIS GIRL FOR MONTHS AND I HAD NO CLUE.
IT'S... WEIRD!

I'M SORRY.
I WAS A SELFISH ASSHOLE FOR NOT TAKING YOUR FEELINGS INTO ACCOUNT.
BESIDES, IT'S NOT LIKE I'M ESPECIALLY PROUD OF THE, UH, SITUATION AND TELLING YOU ONLY WOULD'VE PUT YOU IN THE SAME DILEMMA YOU'RE IN NOW.
PLUS...
(AND, YES, I'M AWARE OF THE IRONY OF WHAT I'M ABOUT TO SAY)
IT'S ALSO, LIKE, A, UM, TRUST THING.
WAIT, "TRUST," AS IN YOU DIDN'T THINK YOU COULD TRUST ME WITH YOUR, UH, SECRET?
NOW MY FEELINGS ARE HURT! WE'RE FRIENDS! I WOULD TELL YOU.
SURE, WE'RE FRIENDS NOW, BUT WHAT IF WE WEREN'T? WHAT IF WE HAD A FALLING OUT?
WHAT IF YOU GOT PISSED OFF AT ME AND TOLD RITU?
I COULDN'T RISK IT.

THAT'S A SHITTY THING TO SAY.
SORRY, MAN, BUT WHEN YOU'RE-- LOOK AT WHAT HAPPENED WITH BROWNIE.
THINGS FALL APART. IT'S SCIENTIFIC.

THE FUNNY PART IS THAT BROWNIE IS ON YOUR SIDE, SAYING MARCY SHOULDN'T TELL RITU. HE--

MARCY CANNOT TELL RITU!!

SHE'S WORRIED THAT IF RITU FINDS OUT SHE'LL BLAME MARCY FOR--
SHE'S NOT GOING TO FIND OUT!
IF MARCY KEEPS QUIET SHE WON'T FIND OUT! IT'S OVER! DONE! THERE'S NOTHING TO FIND OUT!
IF SHE TELLS RITU IT WILL WRECK OUR MARRIAGE. IS THAT WHAT SHE WANTS ??

SHE ISN'T THE ONE--
CAN I ASK YOU ONE QUESTION?
WHY.

I MEAN, SURE, I UNDERSTAND WHY IN, LIKE, THE SAME WAY EVERYONE THINKS ABOUT IT, BUT WHY...
WHAT MADE YOU, UH, PULL THE TRIGGER?

YOU SAID YOU DON'T PLAN ON LEAVING SO--? YOU KNOW WHAT? IT'S NONE OF MY BUSINESS SO YOU
OKAY, I LOVE RITU, OKAY??

BUT LATELY THINGS BETWEEN US HAVE BEEN--
WE'VE ONLY HAD SEX, LIKE, THREE TIMES IN THE LAST YEAR.

OKAYWELLLIKE ISAIDIT'SNOTREALLY ANY OF MYBUSINESS RIGHT SO,UM--

AND, YES, SHE WAS PREGNANT A LOT OF THAT TIME AND THE BABY, I GET IT, BUT THIS, UH, "DRY SPELL" STARTED BEFORE THAT. THIS HAS BEEN, LIKE, YEARS.

I'M NOT REALLY BLAMING HER FOR MY... I KNOW HAVING KIDS CAN CHANGE A WOMAN'S...
BUT, LIKE, WHAT ELSE CAN I DO? BE CELIBATE THE REST OF MY LIFE? JERK OFF LIKE SOME HIGH SCHOOL KID?
YEAH, HUH. WOW.

SO THE WAY I SEE IT I'M REDUCED TO THREE OPTIONS:
STAY FAITHFUL AND RESIGN MYSELF TO A LIFE OF BITTER CHASTITY AND SIMMERING RESENTMENT.
I CAN WALK AWAY FROM TWELVE YEARS OF MARRIAGE, TURNING BRAIDEN AND CHLOE'S LIVES UPSIDE DOWN.
OR I CAN, UH, MAKE OCCASIONAL TRIPS OFF THE RESERVATION.
YEAH, OR OPTION FOUR: KEEP YOUR DAMN DICK IN YOUR TROUSERS AND STOP CHEATING ON YOUR WIFE?!
SLURPP
YEAH, I THOUGHT OF THAT, BUT I DIDN'T WANT HIM TO CLAM UP IF I GOT TOO JUDGMENTAL, SO I JUST RESPONDED WITH VAGUE, NON-COMMITTAL GRUNTS.

AUGHH, HOW ON EARTH ARE WE SUPPOSED TO HAVE DINNER WITH THEM NOW?!
I CAN'T DECIDE WHICH ONE OF THEM I CAN'T LOOK IN THE EYE MORE!
WHY DON'T WE JUST BAIL?
I'M SURE SCOTTY WOULD BE RELIEVED. WE CAN STAY IN AND CATCH UP ON "COMMUNITY".
SCREW SCOTTY! WE SHOULD JUST GO AND DUMP HIS DIRTY LAUNDRY ON THE TABLE!
IF YOU HAD TOLD ME HE WAS, LIKE, ALL REMORSEFUL AND THAT THIS WHOLE THING WAS, LIKE, AN ACT OF IMPULSIVE, UH, LIKE, PASSION AND THAT HE, UM, CRASHED TO HIS KNEES IN REMORSE, I'D--
(WELL, NOT FORGIVE HIM, REALLY)
--BUT I WOULD AT LEAST...
IT WOULD BE MORE UNDERSTANDABLE!
BUT YOU MAKE HIM SOUND LIKE HE WAS, UH, LIKE THIS, YOU KNOW, ALL VULCAN AND ANALYTICAL ABOUT IT!
YOU MAKE IT SOUND LIKE HE DOESN'T REGRET FUCKING AROUND ON RITU AT ALL, LIKE HE'S JUST UPSET AND WORRIED I'LL BUST HIM!

OKAY, WELL I DON'T KNOW WHY YOU'RE GETTING ALL PISSY AT ME, I'M NOT THE ONE WHO CHEATED, OKAY?
I GUESS I'M GETTING "PISSY" BECAUSE YOU'RE ACTING LIKE THIS IS NO BIG DEAL.
?? HOW AM--
IT'S GOING TO CHANGE EVERYTHING BUT YOU GUYS JUST SEEM TO THINK YOU'RE, LIKE, TEENAGERS LIVING A LIFE UTTERLY WITHOUT CONSEQUENCES. SCOTT--
YOU ARE FINISHED? DESSERT?
UM, NO, WE'RE STILL--
OH, I'M SORRY. SORRY.
I'M SORRY, I'M JUST--
I GUESS THIS THING IS MORE, UH, UPSETTING THAN I THOUGHT.
SCREW IT: I'M GONNA CANCEL DINNER. I'LL TELL HER YOU HAVE TO WORK LATE, THAT A SHIH TZU GOT DIAR-RHEA OR SOMETHING.

THE ONE THING THEY DON'T...

LOOK, YOU KNOW I LOVE MY KIDS, RIGHT? I'VE ONLY KNOWN CHLOE FOR A MONTH BUT I WOULD-- I'D TAKE A BULLET FOR HER.

BUT THE ONE THING NO ONE PREPARES YOU FOR IS THAT KIDS AUTOMATICALLY KNOCK THE FATHER TO THE BOTTOM OF THE FOOD CHAIN.

ALL THE ATTENTION MARCY GIVES YOU...

THE KIDS COME FIRST.

AND DON'T GET ME WRONG: THAT'S HOW IT SHOULD BE.

BUT

SOMETIMES YOU REALLY MISS THE BOND YOU HAD WHEN IT WAS JUST THE TWO OF YOU, YOU KNOW?

SOMETIMES IT'S LONELY.

BUT I SUPPOSE THESE ARE THE SACRIFICES WE CHOSE TO MAKE, RIGHT?

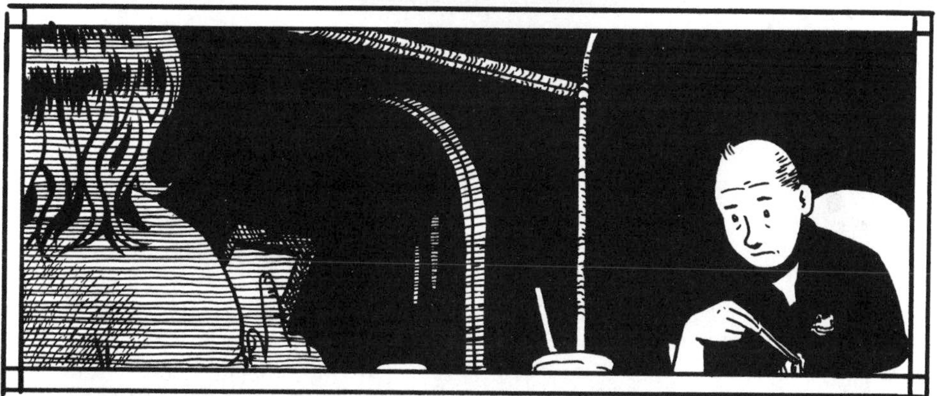

IN 2011, SCIENTISTS OBSERVED A PLANET THAT DOESN'T REVOLVE AROUND A STAR BUT, INSTEAD, ROAMS THE GALAXY ALONE.
WE DON'T KNOW THE STORY WITH THESE "ROGUE" PLANETS.
SOME THINK THEY'RE STARS THAT FAILED TO IGNITE,
OR PLANETS KNOCKED FROM THEIR ORBIT AND HURLED INTO SPACE.
THESE LONE TRAVELERS ARE TOUGH TO SPOT, BUT ONE HYPOTHESIS IS THAT THERE ARE ACTUALLY MORE "ROGUE" PLANETS THAN "NORMAL" ONES.

IMPACT
I, UM...
I JUST...
I'M SORRY, I JUST THOUGHT YOU WOULD... IF, I, UH WAS IN YOUR SHOES I THOUGHT YOU'D, YOU'D WANT TO, TO, UM,
TO KNOW.

Who is SHE??
I DON'T REALLY KNOW. LIKE I SAID, I JUST BUMPED--
THAT ASSHOLE!!
THAT FUCKING SHITBAG ASSHOLE MOTHER FUCKING CHEATING PRICK-FACED ASSHOLE!!
I'M SORRY I HAD TO --
I'M JUST SORRY.
WHAT ARE--
THAT--
GOD DAMN IT! I KNEW IT! I FUCKING KNEW IT!!
MAYBE, I DON'T KNOW, YOU GUYS COULD GET, LIKE, COUNSELING OR...
YEAH, OR MAYBE I CAN GET A GUN AND SHOOT HIS FUCKING... DICK OFF!
HAHA! SHE'S JUST--
CAN WE GET, LIKE, SOME MORE, UH, WATER, OR--?

I SHOULD HAVE KNOWN. EVERY BONE IN MY BODY WAS SCREAMING IT BUT DID I LISTEN? NO.
I'M SUCH AN IDIOT. SUCH AN IDIOT.
COME ON, YOU CAN'T BLAME YOURSELF FOR THIS. HE'S THE IDIOT! HE'S THE ONE WHO--
HE'S THE IDIOT, RIGHT?
YOU SAID SHE WAS BLONDE?
YEAH.
SKINNY?
DON'T SAY SKINNY.
BLONDE.
PSSH. OF COURSE.
WHY AM I SUCH A BITCH?

YOU'RE NOT A-- YOU'RE AWESOME! THIS IS HIS FAULT, RITU! YOU CAN'T BLAME YOURSELF!
YEAH, "FOOL ME ONCE...," RIGHT? (WHERE THE FUCK ARE MY GODDAMN--??)
THERE YOU GO! YOU GUYS WILL--
WAIT, WHAT DO YOU MEAN?
I MEAN THAT WE'VE--
THIS ISN'T THE FIRST TIME, MARCE.
HE'S DONE THIS BEFORE.
...
H-HE HAS?
ONCE.
OR: ONCE I KNOW OF. ANYWAY.
GULP

WHOA.
RITU, I'M SO SORRY THAT THIS... I CAN'T EVEN IMAGINE.
WHAT -- happened?
WHAT HAPPENED THE FIRST TIME I CAUGHT HIM CHEATING?
OR WHAT HAPPENED TO OUR RELATIONSHIP THAT MY HUSBAND FEELS THE NEED TO FUCK OTHER WOMEN?
UM. The...
The first one?
NOTHING.
HE CHEATED. I FOUND OUT. THAT'S ABOUT IT.
OH MY GOD. I'M SO SORRY.
I MEAN, YOU ALWAYS HEAR ABOUT THIS SORT OF THING AND I GUESS IT, LIKE, HAPPENS ALL THE TIME, RIGHT?
BUT, SCOTTY! I NEVER PEGGED HIM AS -- I JUST NEVER THOUGHT OF HIM AS THAT KIND OF GUY, RIGHT?

SO... WHAT ARE YOU GOING TO DO? CONFRONT HIM? GO SEE, LIKE, A MARRIAGE COUNSELOR OR--?
WHY DO YOU KEEP SAYING THAT? ABOUT SEEING A COUNSELOR?
OH, SORRY, I DIDN'T MEAN TO BE--
I JUST THOUGHT, YOU KNOW, YOU GUYS HAVE BEEN TOGETHER A LONG TIME AND I'M SURE YOU CAN WORK THROUGH--
OH! I'M SO GRATEFUL FOR YOUR ADVICE BECAUSE YOU'VE OBVIOUSLY HAD A LOT MORE TIME TO, UH, UH, PROCESS THIS INFORMATION.
Um.
I-I REMEMBER MY PARENTS HAD A
PERSONALLY? I'VE ONLY JUST FOUND OUT A MINUTE AGO, AFTER YOU AND, I ASSUME, BILLY, RIGHT?
PLUS WHOEVER BILLY TOLD, SO, YEAH, I'M, HA
BILLY DIDN'T TELL ANYBODY!
I-I FEEL LIKE YOU'RE GETTING PISSED OFF AT ME AND I--
WOULD YOU RATHER I DIDN'T--

NONO, PLEASE: GO ON! REALLY, TELL ME WHAT YOU THINK I SHOULD DO!
YOU AND BILLY, YOU GUYS HAVE, LIKE, THE PERFECT MARRIAGE SO--
OKAY, YOU KNOW WHAT? YOU'RE OBVIOUSLY UPSET SO I'M JUST GONNA GO.
BUT I'M REALLY SORRY THAT THIS ALL HAPPENED, I LOVE YOU AND IT'S NOT YOUR FAULT.
OH, THANK YOU, YOUR HOLINESS! YOUR, UH, ABSOLUTION WILL REALLY EASE MY--
UM.
I'M SORRY, BUT, UH, HERE'S THAT WATER.
AND A, UH, COOKIE.
NO CHARGE.
TH--
THANK YOU.

BLAST OFF
YOU THINK YOU'RE UP FOR ANOTHER EPISODE WHEN WE GET HOME?
I THINK WE ONLY HAVE TWO LEFT UNTIL WE'RE DONE WITH SEASON FOUR.
OKAY, SO FOR NOW WE'LL JUST SET UP THE CRIB AND STUFF IN OUR ROOM, BUT THAT'S ONLY A SHORT-TERM SOLUTION, RIGHT? 
YEAH, I GUESS SO. WE'LL FIGURE IT OUT.
1030

YEAH, I THOUGHT THAT WAS WHAT WE WERE DOING NOW: FIGURING IT OUT.
BUT I FEEL EVERY TIME WE TALK ABOUT IT YOU -- WE JUST KEEP PUTTING IT OFF. WE --
YEAH, BECAUSE WE HAVE, LIKE, MONTHS TO FIGURE IT OUT BUT... YOU KNOW YOU ALWAYS OVERTHINK STUFF AND GET ANXIOUS ABOUT STUFF THAT'S ALL, LIKE, THEORETICAL.
"THEORETICAL??" WHAT DID
RINGTONE!
UGH, IT'S MISS.
GO AHEAD, YOU CAN TAKE IT.
SCOFF
SHE PROBABLY JUST WANTS TO COMPLAIN ABOUT SOMETHING HER--
Miss
SO BACK TO THE "THEORETICAL" CHILD CURRENTLY GROWING IN MY UTERUS...

OKAY, OKAY, MAYBE I'M NOT USING THE RIGHT, WHATEVER-YOU-CALL-IT, WORD BUT YOU KNOW WHAT I MEAN, MARCE. YOU'RE, LIKE, WORRYING ABOUT STUFF THAT'S SO FAR IN THE FUTURE, IT'S--
DELI
WE HAVE TIME TO SORT ALL THIS OUT SO LET'S TA ONE
"TIME?" WE HAVE SIX MONTHS, BILL, AND WE HAVE, LIKE, A HUNDRED THINGS WE--
WE HAVE TO GO OVER OUR FINANCES, WE HAVE TO START MAKING ROOM FOR STUFF LIKE A CRIB, WE HAVE TO GET A CRIB, A STROLLER, DIAPER STUFF, WE HAVE TO LOOK INTO, UH, MATERNITY LEAVE, LIFE INSURANCE, CHILDBIRTH CLASSES, UH, PEDIATRICIANS, WE HAVE TO BABYPROOF THE--
RINGTONE!
THE KID WON'T EVEN BE ABLE TO CRAWL FOR--
:SIGH: YOUR SISTER'S CALLING ME NOW. YOU SHOULD TAKE IT.
FINE, BUT WE'RE NOT DONE WITH--
MISS? WHAT'S UP? IT'S NOT REALLY A GOOD--

WHAT?? WHAT DO YOU MEAN??
IS SHE OKAY?? WHAT HAPPENED?
OH MY GOD! OH MY GOD! IS SHE OKAY?
SHE--
WERE YOU THERE WHEN IT--
SHIT.
UH-HUH UH-HUH...
WHAT SHOULD.. OKAY, OKAY, SEND US THE ADDRESS AND WE'LL..
NO!!
OKAY, I'LL TEXT YOU WHEN WE.. RIGHT, RIGHT.
UM, OKAY, BYE.

THAT WAS MISS.
(WAIT, WHY ARE MY APPS ALL..?)
I KNOW! WHAT DID SHE SAY??
SHE...
IT'S WEIRD: THE APPS ON MY PHONE ARE ALL, LIKE, IN DIFFERENT PLACES. DID YOU--
THAT'S BECAUSE IT'S MY PHONE!
WHAT DID SHE SAY?? IT SOUNDED..
OH, THAT WAS MISS. SHE SAID MY MOM HAD A STROKE.
OH MY GOD! IS SHE OKAY??
WHAT HAPPENED??
SHE...MISS SAID SHE'S IN THE HOSPITAL.
(MOM'S IN THE HOSPITAL, I MEAN, NOT..)
IT'S TOO EARLY TO REALLY, UM, REALLY -- TO TELL
SHIT! WHAT DO WE DO??
THAT'S...
YEAH, YEAH WE PROBABLY SHOULD...

I'M COUNTING ON YOU, MOMMY!
YOU WRECKED MY MARRIAGE!
TERRIBLE DAUGHTER
YOU'RE A LOUSY FRIEND AND WE ALL TALK ABOUT HOW SAD YOU ARE.
I DON'T WANT SOME STUPID BRAT WRECKING MY LIFE!
exhale!
OKAY: WE NEED TO RENT A CAR SO WE CAN GO OUT TO NEW JERSEY.
DO YOU THINK BROWNIE CAN TAKE CARE OF CHOPS FOR A FEW DAYS?
I'LL CHECK.
ASK FOR THREE NIGHTS. WE'LL MAKE OTHER ARRANGEMENTS IF WE'RE GONE LONGER THAN THAT.
ARE... ARE YOU OKAY?
NO, BUT I'LL DEAL WITH THAT LATER.

THANKS, ELLA, I'LL KEEP YOU POSTED. BYE.
Meat

OKAY, SO I GOT ELLA TO OPEN THE STORE TOMORROW.
LET ME CALL BROWNIE.
YO!

HEY, DUDE, SORRY TO CALL YOU SO LATE.
I--
NO PROBLEM, I WAS JUST WATCHING "POON HOUSE." HAVE YOU SEEN THIS AWFUL SHOW?
CIVILIZATION IS COLLAPSING, MAN.

I WAS ACTUALLY CALLING TO ASK YOU A HUGE FAVOR: WOULD YOU MIND TAKING CARE OF CHOPS FOR A DAY OR TWO?
MARCY'S MOM IS IN THE HOSPITAL AND WE--
WHO CARES IF I'M A ▭NG SLUT?? I DIDN'T COME HERE TO MAKE F▭NG FRIENDS!!
JESUS! IT'S FUCKING NUTS. PEOPLE WILL DO ANYTHING TO BE ON T.V. FAME IS TO AMERICANS WHAT CHRISTIANITY WAS TO MEDIEVAL TIMES. WE'LL DO--

UH-HUH.
SO...

RIGHT, RIGHT.

HE'S LECTURING ME ABOUT OUR MODERN WORLD.

YEAH, SO LISTEN: MARCE AND I ARE ON THE WAY TO THE HOSPITAL SO COULD YOU DO ME A HUGE --
...

NO, NO, IT'S MARCY'S MOM. SHE HAD--
SO, YOU THINK YOU CAN TAKE CARE OF CHOPS FOR--
COOL.
COOL. THANKS, DUDE, I'LL LET YOU KNOW.
LATER.

Whew
ALL SET.
IT'S FUNNY, WHEN I MENTIONED THE HOSPITAL HE ASSUMED IT WAS SOMETHING WRONG WITH THE BABY.
WHEN I TOLD HIM IT WAS ABOUT YOUR, UH, THAT IT HAD NOTHING TO DO WITH THE BABY HE ALMOST SOUNDED DISAPPOINTED.

YEAH, THAT'S HYSTERICAL.

FINALLY! WHAT TOOK YOU GUYS??
REGISTRATIO

HOW IS SHE? IS SHE OKAY??
JIM.
BILL.
OH, MONKEY...

THE DOCTOR SAID SHE'S STABLE BUT IT'S TOO EARLY TO TELL HOW BAD IT IS.
WE'RE ABOUT TO GO UP AND SEE HER.

THEY SAID SHE WAS IN THE PARKING LOT OF MEGA-LO-MART WHEN SOMEONE SAW HER FALL OVER!
WE NEEDED MILK. I-- I SHOULDN'T'VE LET HER GO ALONE! I--

IT'S OKAY, RUSS.
THEY SAID WE WERE LUCKY, IN A WAY: ANOTHER FEW MINUTES AND SHE WOULD'VE BEEN DRIVING WHEN IT HAPPENED.
FUN RUN
UNCLE BILLY!!

HEY, MUGS, HOW'S IT GOING? YOU HOLDING UP OKAY?
CAN WE GO HOME YET?? THIS PLACE IS SO BORING AND IT FUCKING SMELLS.
OOH! I'M TELLING MOM YOU SAID EFF-YOO-SEE-KAY!!
BLOOD DRIVE
CTOR SAID SHE DOING?
94
UNCLE BILLY, CAN WE PLAY SKULL ATTACK? MOM SAID IT WAS OKAY!!
SURE, TUCK. AND DON'T WORRY ABOUT GRAMMY. THE DOCTOR'S AD EVERYTHI
I GO FIRST.
NO WAY!! I AXED FIRST!
LET GO, PIGDICK! YOU'RE MESSING ME UP SO I GOTTA START OVER!!
C'MON! GIVE IT! UNCLE BILLY, I AXED SO I SHOULD MAKE HIM GIVE IT TO ME!!
QUIT IT
C'MON!
GIVE IT!!
QUIT IT!
BOYS

BUSTED!
FINE, BABY!
WE'LL TAKE TURNS!
CAN YOU SHOW ME HOW TO GET PAST THE BIG PLANT?
"WAIT 'TIL HE CLOSES HIS MOUTH AFTER THE THIRD BITE."
GRAB THAT COIN.
I KNOW!!
UNCLE BILLY, YOU KNOW WHAT HAPPENED?
MY FRIEND TY GOT, LIKE, FIVE MILLION POINTS AND YOU KNOW WHAT HAPPENED?
GASP! I GOT HIM!
IT, LIKE, TOTALLY FRIED HIS IPHONE!
IT'S TRUE! HE BROUGHT IT TO SCHOOL AND THE SCREEN WAS ALL, LIKE, CRACKED!!
REALLY? HE MUST'VE BEEN PIS-- ANGRY!
HE WASN'T 'CUZ YOU KNOW WHY?
IF THAT HAPPENS YOU SEND IT TO THE GAME COMPANY AND THEY SEND YOU, LIKE, A BRAND NEW PHONE WITH, LIKE, UNLIMITED LIVES!
SHOOT! I'VE NEVER MADE IT THIS FAR!! HOW--
AW, MAN...
MY TURN!!!

UNCLE BILLY, CAN I GET A SIGGLY BAR FROM THE CANDY MACHINE??
MY MOM SAID I COULD!
OH, SHE DID, DID SHE?
HMM, I ONLY HAVE TWENTIES...
OBEY
Beep
Bloop
Bloop
CRACK!
SO, MOM IS AWAKE. THEY SAID WE CAN GO UP AND SEE HER.

9047
LEVEL 7

THAT'S GREAT! I'LL STAY DOWN HERE WITH THESE GUYS.
AUNTIE M, CAN WE HAVE SOME MONEY TO GET CANDY FROM THE CANDY MACHINE?
MY MOM SAID WE COULD!

YEAH, DO YOU HAVE ANY SMALL BILLS FOR THE VENDING MACHINE?
WE'LL BE UP IN ROOM 314.
THANNNK YOU!

CLICK
CLACK

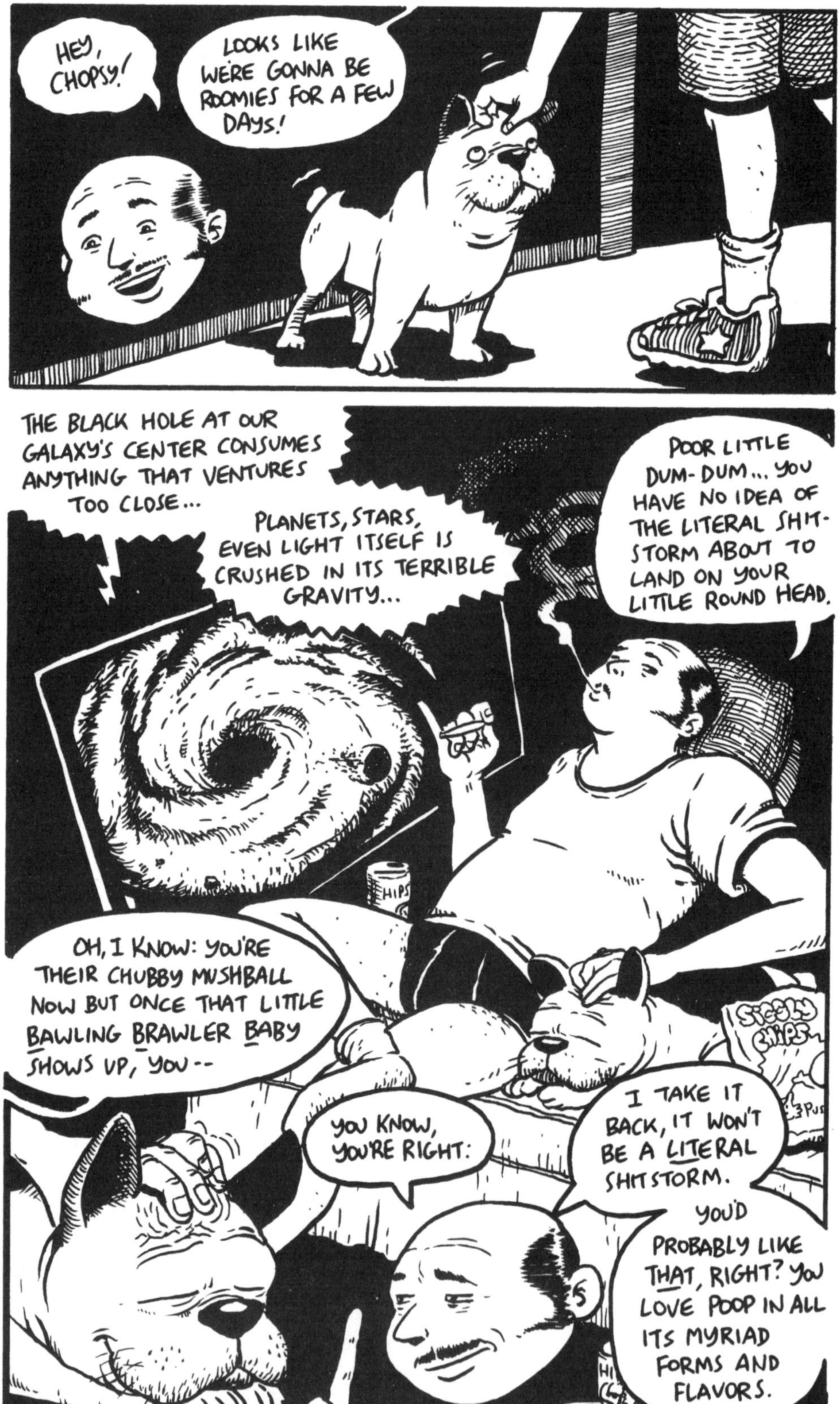

THE BLACK HOLE AT OUR GALAXY'S CENTER CONSUMES ANYTHING THAT VENTURES TOO CLOSE...

PLANETS, STARS, EVEN LIGHT ITSELF IS CRUSHED IN ITS TERRIBLE GRAVITY...

POOR LITTLE DUM-DUM... YOU HAVE NO IDEA OF THE LITERAL SHIT-STORM ABOUT TO LAND ON YOUR LITTLE ROUND HEAD.

OH, I KNOW: YOU'RE THEIR CHUBBY MUSHBALL NOW BUT ONCE THAT LITTLE BAWLING BRAWLER BABY SHOWS UP, YOU--

YOU KNOW, YOU'RE RIGHT:

I TAKE IT BACK, IT WON'T BE A LITERAL SHITSTORM.

YOU'D PROBABLY LIKE THAT, RIGHT? YOU LOVE POOP IN ALL ITS MYRIAD FORMS AND FLAVORS.

YOU WOULDN'T BE THE FIRST BELOVED PET KICKED TO THE CURB WHEN THE BABY COMES.
SAD TO SAY.
DON'T GET ME WRONG: I'M SURE THEY HAVE EVERY INTENTION OF KEEPING YOU AND FIGURING IT OUT SOMEHOW.
YOU DON'T WANT TO GO DEVELOPING ANY OF YOUR PATENTED MYSTERY RASHES OR UNEXPLAINED BREATHING PROBLEMS.
THE GOOD NEWS IS THAT THEY PROBABLY WON'T EVEN NOTICE.
BUT TRUST ME: DON'T MAKE THEM CHOOSE BETWEEN A VET BILL OR NEVAEH'S PRE-K MUSIC CLASSES.
IT'S ALMOST TRAGIC, SINCE I KNOW HOW MUCH YOU ADORE THEM. THEY'RE LIKE THE CENTER OF YOUR LITTLE WORLD.
To Be Donated
To Be Donated
MY HEART GOES OUT TO YOU, OLD PAL.

WHAT ARE YOU GETTING? CHIPS?
I WAS GONNA BUT THEY ONLY HAVE BARBEQUE AND CLAM.
GET SOMETHING FOR ELIJAH, TOO.
LET'S SEE...
BULLY BARS
ENERGY
BLECH.
NO.
METEOR BITES
CANDY
I CAN'T PICK BETWEEN CANDY OR SALTY.
NAH.
HOW ABOUT YUM-YUM TARTS?
NO WAY! THOSE ARE SO GROSS. THEY SHOULD CALL THEM "DUM-DUM FARTS!"

PET THERAPY 217
RADIOLOGY 69
ELIJAH, WHAT DO THOSE BLUE LINES AT THE BOTTOM MEAN?
DON'T TOUCH.

THE TOP ONE TEL
HOW MANY ENERGY
HAVE LEFT, THE BO
LIVES YOU HAVE

DOUBLE-CL
EXTRA POINTS
BONUS LEVE

HAHA! NEVER GE LEVEL IF DO IT?

HIGH SCORE SO COOL! MY ROCCO GOT 20, RED LEVEL?
NO WAY.

SCRUNCH SCRUNCH SCRUNCH SCRUNCH SCRUNCH SCRUNCH
GULP

OKAY, KIDS. I THINK IT'S TIME WE WENT UP TO--
QUIT IT!
LET GO, DICKWAD! I'M STILL GOING!
YOU STARTED A NEW ONE! I NEVER--
GOD, WHY DO YOU HAVE TO BE SUCH A FUCKING BABY??
I'M NOT A BABY! AND I'M TELLING MOM YOU SAID--

BOYS.

LET'S GO UP AND SEE YOUR GRAMMY.
BUT...
WE TOLD THEM WE WOULD BE WAITING DOWN HERE.

LISTEN... ELIJAH...
I KNOW HOSPITALS ARE GROSS AND WEIRD AND KINDA, LIKE, SCARY, AND YOU'D RATHER JUST HANG OUT DOWN HERE PLAYING VIDEO GAMES, BUT...
THERE ARE TIMES IN YOUR LIFE WHERE YOU HAVE TO JUST FACE THE GROSS, WEIRD SCARINESS AND JUST, LIKE, DO IT, Y'KNOW? IT'S PART OF, LIKE, GROWING UP.
I KNOW IT WOULD MEAN A LOT TO HER, IF WE WENT UP AND JOINED THE REST OF THE FAMILY.
AND, TRUST ME: YOU'RE GONNA SEE THAT WHEN YOU FACE SOMETHING YOU'RE SCARED OF IT CAN BE..
ALRIGHT ALREADY! I'LL GO UP IF IT MEANS YOU'LL STOP BORING ME TO DEATH WITH THIS FUCKING LECTURE! GOD!!

28-IF

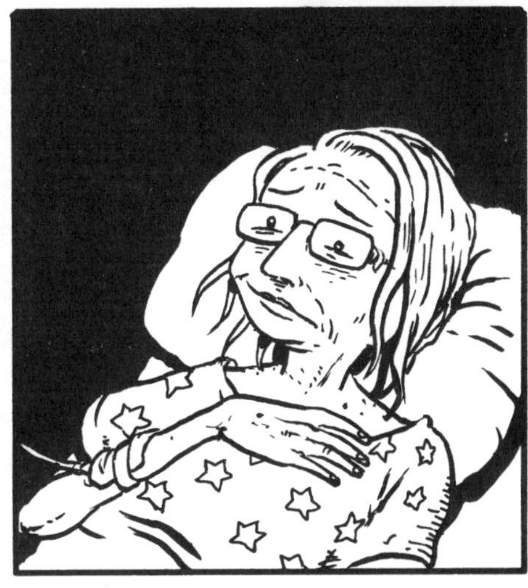

IN 6,000,000,000 YEARS. THE SUN WILL BEGIN TO CONSUME THE LAST OF ITS NUCLEAR FUEL AND SWELL TO 200 TIMES ITS PRESENT SIZE.

FINALLY... ...UTTERLY SPENT, IT WILL SHED ITS OUTER LAYERS, LEAVING ONLY A DENSE, COOLING CINDER LESS THAN ONE-PERCENT ITS CURRENT SIZE.

The "Biggest Gift"
HEY.
HEY!

I WONDER HOW GLOBAL WARMING WILL AFFECT THE LEAVES CHANGING COLOR.
IF I HAD TO GUESS... NEGATIVELY?

I KNOW CLIMATE CHANGE GETS A BAD RAP IN THE MAINSTREAM MEDIA BUT THERE MUST BE SOME PLUSSES, RIGHT?

SUNSCREEN COMPANIES PROBABLY LIKE IT.

EXACTLY! I'M SURE THE DINOSAURS WERE BUMMED OUT BY THAT ASTEROID, BUT IT ALSO CLEARED THE WAY FOR US, RIGHT?
SO THE POSITIVE SIDE OF GLOBAL WARMING IS THAT IT WILL WIPE OUT THE HUMANS?

YOU GOTTA FIND YOUR SILVER LININGS WHERE YOU CAN, MAN.

OH, AND SPEAKING OF NATURAL DISASTERS, HAVE YOU SEEN SCOTTY LATELY? HOW ARE THEY HOLDING UP AFTER CHEATERGATE?
"CHEATERGATE?" YOU CAN DO BETTER THAN THAT.
UM, IT'S HARD TO SAY.
THAT SOUNDS INTRIGUING. DISH.
HA, WELL DON'T GET TOO EXCITED. THEY'RE STILL TOGETHER.
MARCE AND I WENT TO DINNER AT THEIR PLACE LAST WEEK.
THAT'S IT? WHAT WAS SO HARD TO SAY ABOUT THAT??
COME ON, HE WAS ONE OF MY BEST FRIENDS. I WANT TO HEAR HOW MISERABLE HE IS!!

IT WAS THE FIRST TIME WE'D HUNG OUT SINCE, UH, THE INCIDENT. WE HADN'T SEEN EACH OTHER FOR A FEW WEEKS AND IT WAS... WEIRD?

YOU BUST MY BALLS ABOUT "CHEATERGATE" WHEN YOU'RE CALLING IT "THE INCIDENT?" FEH.

STRAINED. EVEN LEAVING ASIDE WHATEVER INTERNAL ISSUES SCOTTY AND RITU ARE SORTING OUT, I THINK THEY'RE BOTH PISSED OFF AT MARCY.

I THINK THEY MUST BLAME HER FOR BRINGING THE WHOLE THING UP.

"OKAY, YOU KNOW HOW FROM TIME TO TIME THE CONVERSATION BREAKS UP ALONG GENDER LINES? SCOTTY AND I GOT INTO A DEBATE ABOUT WHICH STAR TREK MOVIE WAS SET IN SAN FRANCISCO AND RITU LISTENED TO US THE WHOLE TIME, EVEN AFTER MARCY BROUGHT UP PREGNANCY STUFF."

DELI
LOTTERY
WOW, SHE IS PISSED.
(AND IT'S STAR TREK II, OF COURSE)
DON'T LET'S START.
YEAH, SO IT'S BEEN VARYING DEGREES OF AWKWARD.
LöBRAU BEER

I THINK I'M GONNA TRY "BUSHWICK GOLD."

HMM. "LAIKA." BREWED IN KUDRYAVKA?
FIRST TIME FOR EVERYTHING.

CHEERS.
SO DO YOU KNOW WHAT THE FALLOUT WAS FROM "THE INCIDENT?"
HAVE YOU TALKED WITH SCOTTY IN A NON-COUPLES FORMAT?
CLINK!
AHH, WE KEEP TALKING ABOUT MAKING PLANS BUT IT JUST NEVER HAPPENS.
YOU KNOW HOW IT IS SOMETIMES.

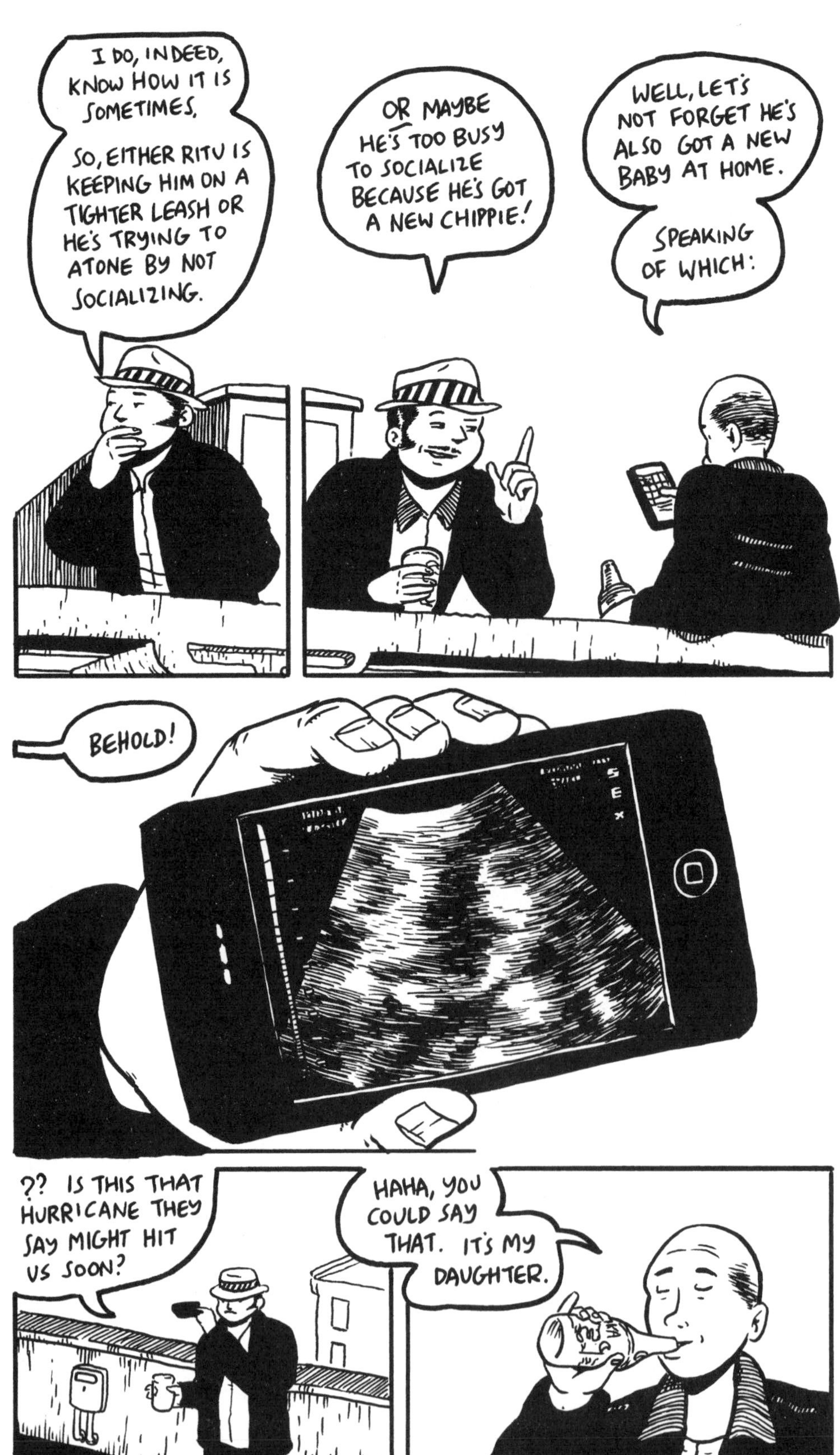
I DO, INDEED, KNOW HOW IT IS SOMETIMES.
SO, EITHER RITU IS KEEPING HIM ON A TIGHTER LEASH OR HE'S TRYING TO ATONE BY NOT SOCIALIZING.
OR MAYBE HE'S TOO BUSY TO SOCIALIZE BECAUSE HE'S GOT A NEW CHIPPIE!
WELL, LET'S NOT FORGET HE'S ALSO GOT A NEW BABY AT HOME.
SPEAKING OF WHICH:
BEHOLD!
SEX
?? IS THIS THAT HURRICANE THEY SAY MIGHT HIT US SOON?
HAHA, YOU COULD SAY THAT. IT'S MY DAUGHTER.

AH, OKAY, I SEE.
REMEMBER THOSE "MAGIC EYE" THINGS? DO THEY STILL MAKE THOSE THINGS?
YEAH, NOT LONG NOW.
WE'VE EVEN NARROWED IT DOWN TO SEVEN NAMES.
WOW. WHAT ARE THEY?
YOU KNOW I CAN'T TELL YOU THAT.
LEMME SEE:
--EMMA
--OLIVIA
--AVA
--AUBREY
...UH..
--LILY
HOW MANY IS THAT? DID I SAY AVA?
CAN I OFFER UP A SUGGESTION? HOW ABOUT CARSON?
"CARSON?"
I DON'T GET IT. WHAT'S THE GAG?

NO, NO GAG. THERE WAS THAT AUTHOR, CARSON McCULLERS. I ALWAYS THOUGHT IT WAS A UNIQUE GIRL'S NAME.
WHAT'S SO FUNNY?

WHAT? NOTHING. IT'S NICE.

IT'S, UH, ALSO LIKE THE SEVENTH MOST POPULAR NAME FOR GIRLS AT THE MOMENT, SO, UH, NOT SO SURE ABOUT THE "UNIQUE" PART THESE DAYS.

WHAT?? REALLY?
UGH! YOU BREEDERS RUIN EVERYTHING!
HA HA!

OKAY, SO...
SO LISTEN: IF IT EVER COMES TO A POINT WHERE YOU AND MARCY HAVE TO GIVE UP CHOPS FOR ANY REASON, I, UH, I WANT TO TAKE HIM. I'LL TAKE HIM.

WAIT: WHY ARE WE GIVING UP CHOPS?
I DON'T KNOW, MAYBE YOU MOVE INTO A NON-PET FRIENDLY CO-OP, MAYBE CARSON IS ALLERGIC, WHO KNOWS?
I'M SURE THINGS ARE GOING TO WORK OUT FINE, BUT JUST IN CASE IT DOESN'T I WANTED TO, YOU KNOW, LET YOU KNOW WHERE I STAND.
I'LL ADMIT I'M GONNA MISS THE LITTLE INBRED MUTANT.
I'M... I'M TOUCHED.
YOU REALLY THINK ONE DAY WE'LL BE ABLE TO AFFORD TO LIVE IN A CO-OP?
UM, I GUESS IN THAT PARTICULAR SCENARIO MARCY REMARRIED AFTER YOUR DEATH.
HA, YEAH, THAT SOUNDS ABOUT RIGHT.
BUT LISTEN: UNTIL THEN WE AREN'T GOING ANYWHERE. YOU'RE WELCOME TO VISIT HIM ANYTIME.
YOU CAN EVEN WALK HIM!

YOU SAY THAT NOW...
(WE SHOULD'VE GOT MORE BEERS.)
AND LISTEN, I KNOW YOU THINK THAT THIS KID IS GOING TO CHANGE EVERYTHING BUT IT..

:Sigh: YOU KNOW WHAT? FORGET WHAT I WAS ABOUT TO SAY: IT IS GOING TO CHANGE EVERYTHING.
BUT YOU'RE INTO ALL THAT COSMIC SHIT SO YOU KNOW BETTER THAN ANYONE THAT CHANGE IS THE NATURAL STATE OF THE WORLD, RIGHT?

LIKE TAYLOR DAYNE TAUGHT US, "You Can't Fight Fate."
BUT YOU KNOW WHAT ELSE? WE'RE BROS.

UGH, PLEASE DON'T USE THAT
IS THERE GOING TO BE AN ADJUSTMENT PERIOD? SURE.
WILL I OCCASIONALLY GET TEARY-EYED WHEN I TALK ABOUT CARSON TAKING HER FIRST STEPS? PROBABLY.

BUT! AM I STILL GOING TO COME OVER FOR A BONG HIT WHEN A NEW CARNAGE WORLD OR MAXIMUM KILL GAME IS RELEASED?
YOU CAN BET ON IT, PAL.
MAX KILL 4 IS SLATED FOR MARCH.

YOU'RE FORCING ME TO EXPRESS EMOTIONS WE NORMALLY KEEP SAFE-LY HIDDEN BEHIND BALL BUSTING AND KUBRICK TRIVIA, BUT...

BROWNIE, I ALWAYS HAVE BEEN, AND ALWAYS SHALL BE, YOUR FRIEND.
SO, WHAT DO YOU SAY, YOU SAPPY BASTARD?
WILL YOU JOIN ME IN A SOLEMN PLEDGE OF ETERNAL BROTHERHOOD?

SURE.
WHAT WAS THAT? I COULDN'T QUITE HEAR...
SURE! SURE!
I'LL JOIN YOU IN YOUR DUMB OLD PLEDGE OF INFERNAL RUTHERFORD. Heh Heh.

MY MAN.
ON ME!
OKAY, WHAT DO YOU SAY WE GRAB SOME DINNER AT ABETTI'S?
ROOF

NEXT STOP: THE CAL-ZONE!
THAT REMINDS ME: DID YOU SEE THOSE ADS FOR THAT ABSURD NEW COMET BURGER?
HALF A POUND OF BEEF AND HALF A POUND OF BACON! PLUS CHEESE!
AMERICA IS NUTS.

MY THEORY IS THAT AS A NATION OF IMMIGRANTS WE FEEL A DEEP EMPTINESS WE TRY TO--
WHAT'S WRONG?
HMM.

NO, I WAS JUST IMAGINING THE IMPACT OF CARSON HANGING OUT WITH HER CRAZY UNCLE BROWNIE AND WONDERING IF I WASN'T TOO HASTY WITH MY PLEDGE.
ROOF

HAHA, WELL I PROMISE I WON'T BE TOO MUCH OF A CORRUPTING--
CLUNK
KEEP CLOSED

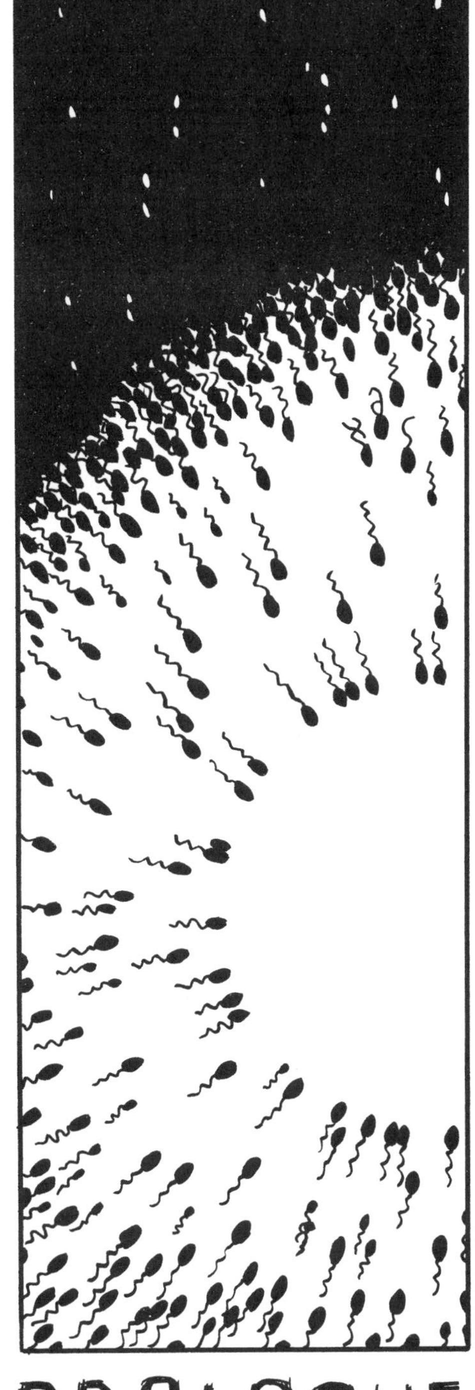

PROLOGUE

COME ON! THINK OF HOW MUCH FUN IT WOULD BE! HIS LITTLE FACE ALL SMOOSHED UP IN BED WITH US...
PLUS, I CAN BRING HIM TO WORK. IT'S WIN-WIN!
BZZZZ!

I DON'T KNOW. SHOULDN'T WE CONSIDER ADOPTION FIRST? THAT'S A LOT OF MONEY. EVEN YOU HAVE TO ADMIT THAT.

BUT I KNOW THE GUY. HE COMES IN ALL THE TIME! I'M SURE HE WOULD CUT ME A DEAL!

HE IS CUTE. I NEVER THOUGHT OF MYSELF AS A DOG PERSON, YOU KNOW?
327
I'LL WEAR YOU DOWN AND ONE DAY YOU'LL THANK ME.

HEY! SORRY, WE COULDN'T HEAR THE BUZZER.
COME ON OUT BACK. KEVIN AND LISA ARE ALREADY HERE.
I BROUGHT MY FAMOUS SALAD, AS REQUESTED!

HEY, GUYS!
YOU'RE JUST IN TIME: BROWNIE WAS JUST LECTURING US ON THE POSITIVE EFFECTS OF PORNOGRAPHY!
IT WASN'T A "LECTURE!"
ALL I WAS SAYING IS THAT IF I WAS A LADY I WOULD MUCH RATHER MY HUSBAND BE LOOKING AT CHUBBY MAMAS DOT NET OR WHATEVER THAN TOM-CATTING AROUND WITH REAL LIFE GIRLS!
SPEAKING OF WHICH: WE BROUGHT SOME KIELBASA FROM POLISH TOM'S!
AWESOMESAUCE! LET'S SLAP THOSE WIENERS ON THE FIRE!
JESUS, WHEN I THINK ABOUT ALL THE MONEY I USED TO THROW AWAY BUYING PORN OVER THE YEARS.
I COULD'VE OWNED A USED DOMESTIC CAR!
THIS WAS IN MY SWINGING SINGLE DAYS, NATCH.

THAT'S REALLY GO
MMM...
CAN YOU PASS THAT SALT? THANKS.
LAST YEAR
OOH, I SEE YOU GOT THE "FANCY" KET
GREY POUPO
WOW
YEAH, WE GOT THEM AT THE FARMER'S MARKET IN RED HOOK.
ANY M ICED TE
HA HA HA!
YOU'RE KIDDING!! OH MY GOD!
THEN NO ONE SHOULD BE ALLOWED TO GET ONE, RIGHT?
OOH! LET ME HAVE SOME OF THAT CORN ON THE COB.!
BUT T MEANS YOU
OH, I LOVE THAT SONG!
HAHA!
MMM
NO WAY, I WOULD NEVER DO THAT
DO YOU REALLY THINK AMERICA WOULD A WOMAN?
YEAH, THANKS FOR HOSTING, GUYS.
URP!
GROSS!
SURE, JUST NOT HER!
MMM
YOU GUYS REALLY DID A BANG UP JOB WITH THIS.
LIKE SCENE IN GODFATHER
NICE W GRILL, SCOTTY.
YEAH, SERIOUSLY
SO GOOD.
STUFFE
THINK I COULD EAT ANOTHER BITE!

OKAY, NOW THAT YOU'RE ALL IN FOOD COMAS WE'LL GET TO THE REASON WE INVITED YOU OVER.

OTHER THAN YOUR CHARMING COMPANY, OF COURSE.

SO... OUR BIG ANNOUNCEMENT IS THAT...

WE'RE PREGNANT.

OH MY GOD, THAT'S SO COOL!! WHEN ARE YOU DUE? HOW FAR ALONG ARE YOU? ARE YOU GOING TO FIND OUT THE SEX? HAVE YOU PICKED OUT NAMES? ARE YOU DOING, LIKE, BIRTHING CLASSES? HAVE YOU TOLD YOUR PARENTS? DO YOU GET MATERNITY LEAVE CAN I TOUCH YOUR STOMACH?

HOLY SHIT, MAN, THAT'S CRAZY. I GUESS YOU GUYS ARE REALLY DOING IT.
SURE SEEMS THAT WAY.
TRUTH BE TOLD, I WAS GETTING A LITTLE NERVOUS. WE'VE BEEN TRYING FOR A WHILE.
WORRIED ABOUT THE OL' BABY BATTER, EH? YOU MUST BE RELIEVED THEN.

HAHA, RIGHT.
THE HARD PART IS OVER: NOW ALL I HAVE TO DO IS RAISE A HUMAN BEING TO ADULTHOOD WITHOUT SCREWING IT UP TOO MUCH, RIGHT?

"YOU WERE LOOKING FOR A JOB AND THEN YOU FOUND A JOB..."

WELL, CONGRATS AGAIN.
OH, SPEAKING OF KIDS: HAVE YOU EVER PLAYED BOX BALL?

BOX--? OH, YOU MEAN THAT GAME WITH THE--?
SURE, THOUGH WE CALLED IT FOUR-SQUARE. WHY?

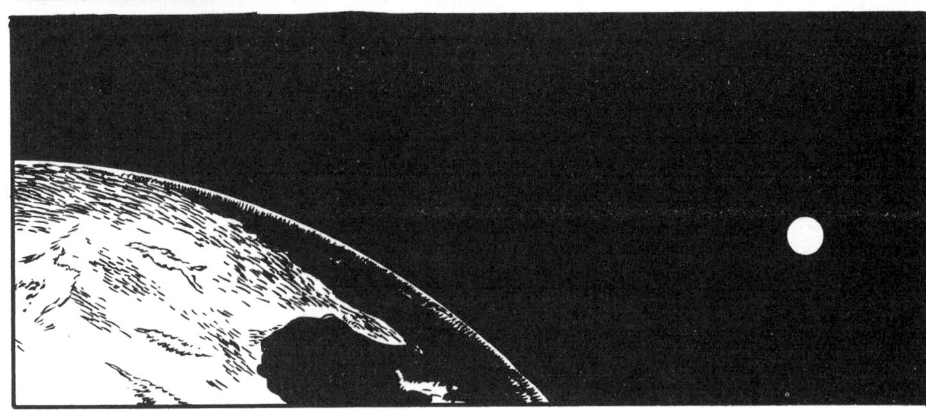

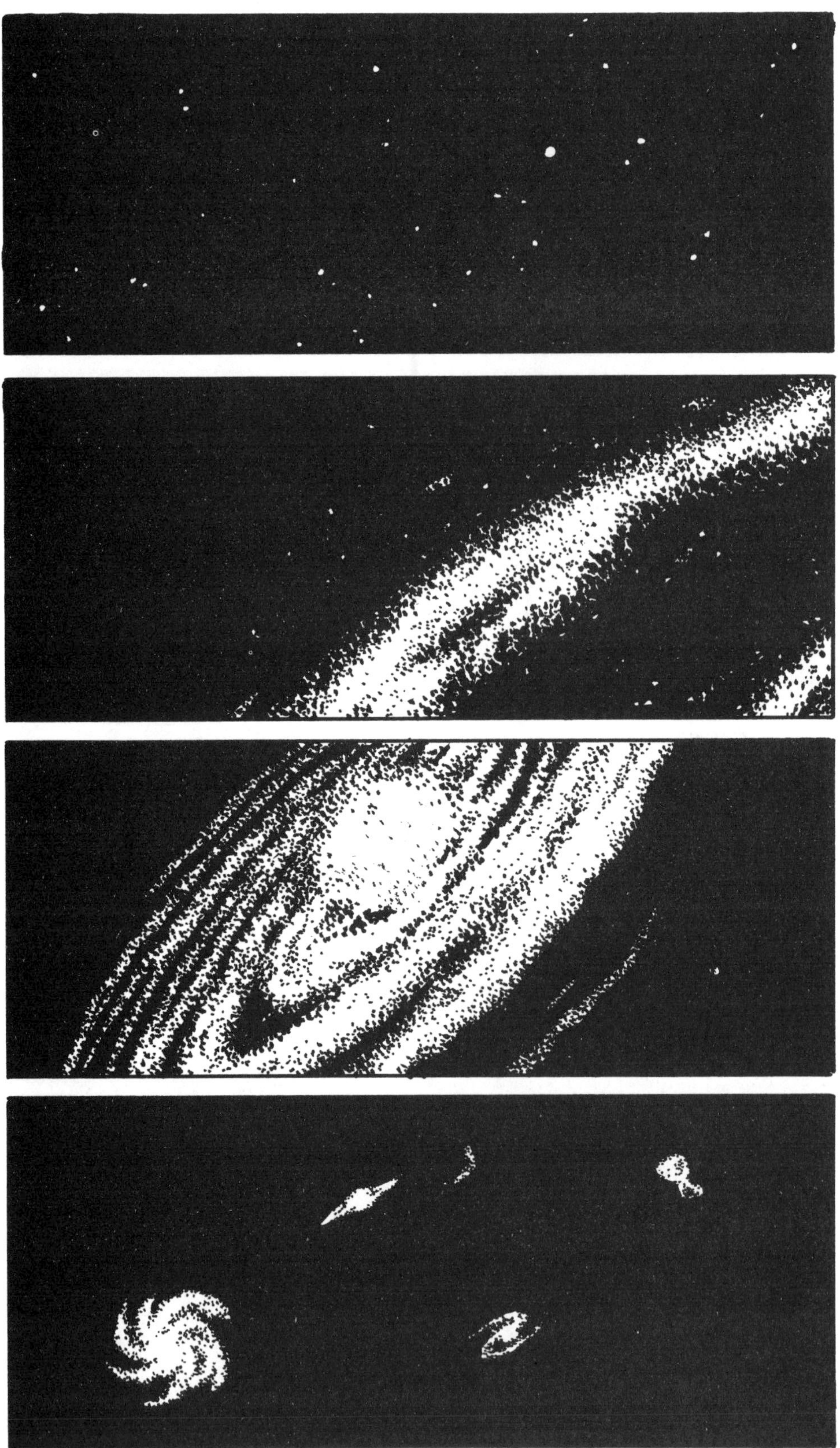

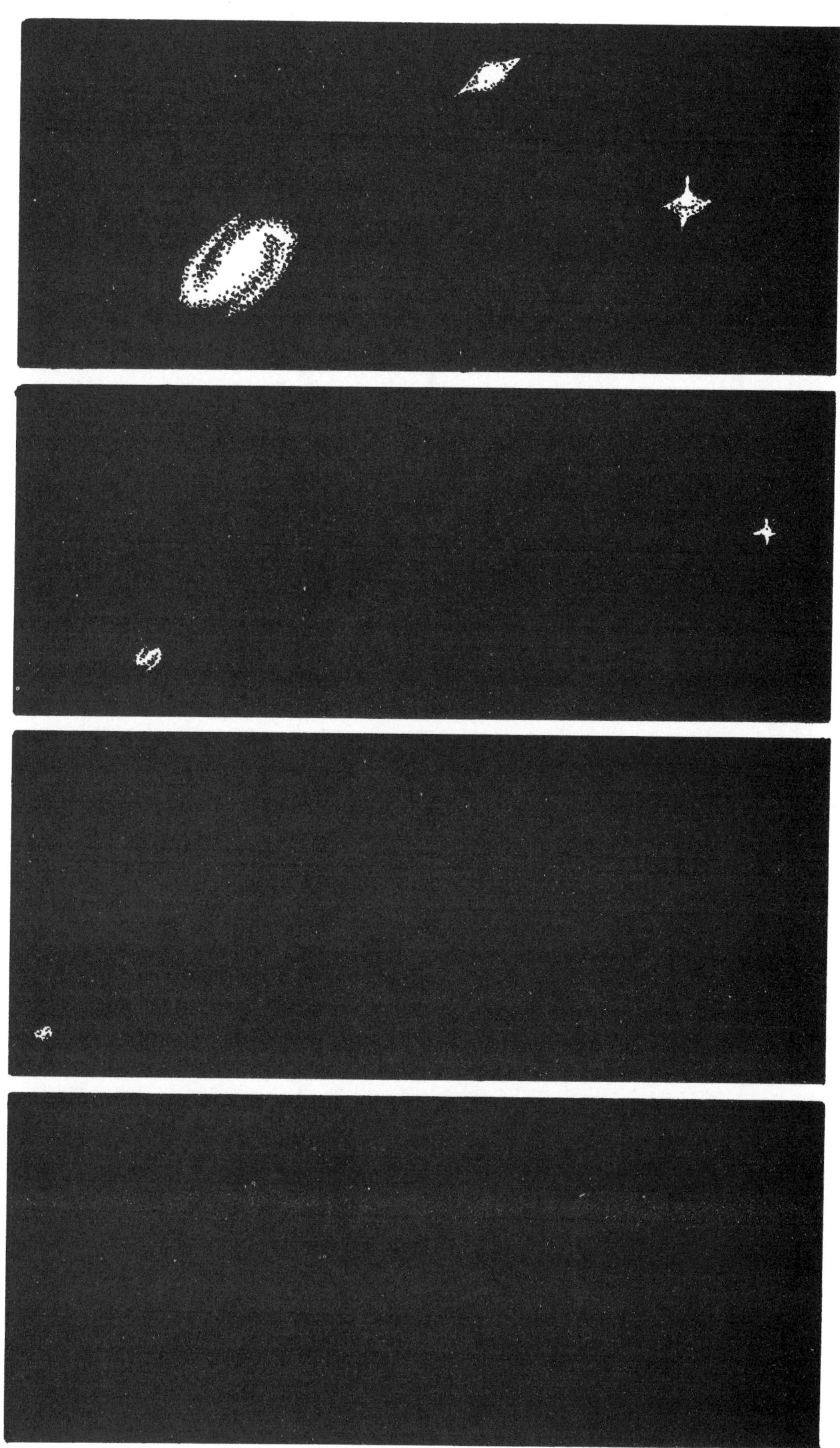

THIS BOOK WOULD NOT HAVE BEEN POSSIBLE WITHOUT THE LOVE AND SUPPORT OF MY PATIENT WIFE KRISTEN SIEBECKER SO I DEDICATE IT TO HER ♡

THANKS TO THE TOP SHELF TEAM, ESPECIALLY CHRIS STAROS CHRIS ROSS LEIGH WALTON

PODCASTS: STAR WARS MINUTE ALPHABEATICAL INK PANTHERS

MY OTHER GRAPHIC NOVELS: BOX OFFICE POISON (2001) TRICKED (2005) ALEX ROBINSON'S LOWER REGIONS (2007) TOO COOL TO BE FORGOTTEN (2008) A KIDNAPPED SANTA CLAUS (with L. FRANK BAUM) (2009)

R.I.P. KRIMPET (1994?-2012)

THANKS TO JOE DAVIDSON FOR HIS PRODUCTION ASSISTANCE

YOU CAN FIND ME ON THE INTERNET AT WWW.COMICBOOKALEX.COM

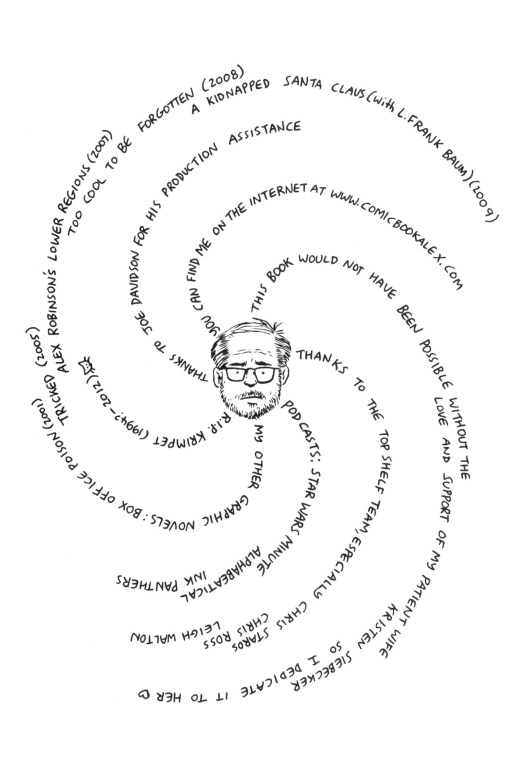